PUERTO RICO

WHAT EVERYONE NEEDS TO KNOW®

PUERTO RICO

WHAT EVERYONE NEEDS TO KNOW®

JORGE DUANY

OXFORD
UNIVERSITY PRESS

OXFORD
UNIVERSITY PRESS

Oxford University Press is a department of the University of Oxford. It furthers the University's objective of excellence in research, scholarship, and education by publishing worldwide. Oxford is a registered trade mark of Oxford University Press in the UK and certain other countries.

"What Everyone Needs to Know" is a registered trademark of Oxford University Press.

Published in the United States of America by Oxford University Press 198 Madison Avenue, New York, NY 10016, United States of America.

Library of Congress Cataloging-in-Publication Data
Title: Puerto Rico : what everyone needs to know / by Jorge Duany.
Description: New York, NY : Oxford University Press, 2017. |
Includes bibliographical references and index.
Identifiers: LCCN 2016046534| ISBN 9780190648701 (paperback) |
ISBN 9780190648695 (hardback) | ISBN 9780190648718 (PDF) |
ISBN 9780190648725 (ePub)
Subjects: LCSH: Puerto Rico—History. | Puerto Rico—Colonization. | Puerto
Rico—Relations—United States. | United States— Relations—Puerto Rico. |
Puerto Rico—Politics and government. | Cultural pluralism—Puerto Rico. |
Puerto Ricans—Migrations. | BISAC: TRAVEL / Caribbean & West Indies. |
HISTORY / Caribbean & West Indies / Cuba.
Classification: LCC F1971 .D83 2017 | DDC 972.95—dc23
LC record available at https://lccn.loc.gov/2016046534

CONTENTS

2 Puerto Rico under US Rule, 1898–1952   43

ACKNOWLEDGMENTS

As usual, I am happy to recognize the steadfast support of my immediate family members—my wife, Diana, and my children, Patricia and Jorge Andrés. Diana has accompanied and encouraged me throughout my academic career over the past three decades, and Patricia and Jorge Andrés have always understood and nurtured my intellectual pursuits. For that, I am forever grateful and hope they all enjoy reading what I have written here, for they are very much a part of the story. To Diana, I can only reiterate that I was blessed when she took Ruth's oath during our wedding many moons ago: "Where you go I will go."

My present colleagues at the Cuban Research Institute of Florida International University have facilitated my work on this and several other projects. I have been fortunate to collaborate with a fine administrative staff, composed of Sebastián Arcos, Aymee Correa, Paola Salavarria, Lennie Gómez, Alfredo González, and Daylen Fiallo. I look forward to continuing our research agenda and public programming in the coming years.

I would also like to acknowledge the intellectual sustenance and solidarity of my former colleagues at the University of Puerto Rico, Río Piedras, especially the Department of Sociology and Anthropology. Among my closest collaborators, I would single out Juan José Baldrich, Jorge Giovannetti, Emilio Pantojas, Lanny Thompson, Luisa Hernández, César A. Rey,

Luz del Alba Acevedo, and María del Carmen Baerga. While I was Acting Dean of the College of Social Sciences at UPR, I had the privilege of working with the dream team of Maritza Barreto, Rebeca Guadalupe, Miriam Febres, and Nilia Manso.

Throughout the years, I have learned much from many insightful scholars of Puerto Rico and its diaspora, some of whom I consider good friends. In addition to those named above, they include Elizabeth Aranda, Jossianna Arroyo, César Ayala, Rafael Bernabe, Jorge Luis Chinea, Arlene Dávila, Grace Dávila, Luis A. Figueroa, Eileen J. Suárez Findlay, Nilda Flores-González, Myrna García-Calderón, Isar P. Godreau, Lillian Guerra, Carmen Dolores Hernández, Guillermo Irizarry, Lawrence La Fountain-Stokes, Teresita A. Levy, Yolanda Martínez-San Miguel, Félix V. Matos-Rodríguez, Edgardo Meléndez, Edwin Meléndez, Nancy Morris, Gina Pérez, Fernando Picó, Ana Yolanda Ramos-Zayas, Carmen Haydée Rivera, Raquel Z. Rivera, Yeidy Rivero, Francisco Scarano, Patricia Silver, Maura Toro-Morn, and Carlos Vargas-Ramos. I have cited some of their work in my suggestions for further reading at the end of this book.

Finally, I would like to thank my former editor at Oxford University Press, Marcela Maxfield, for inviting me to write this book, expertly guiding me through the initial stages of the project, and providing excellent feedback on an earlier version of the book manuscript. Angela Chnapko took over the last phases of the process at OUP, and I appreciate her diligent support and useful recommendations as well. Sasirekka Gopalakrishnan did a wonderful job coordinating the production, copyediting, and proofreading of the book.

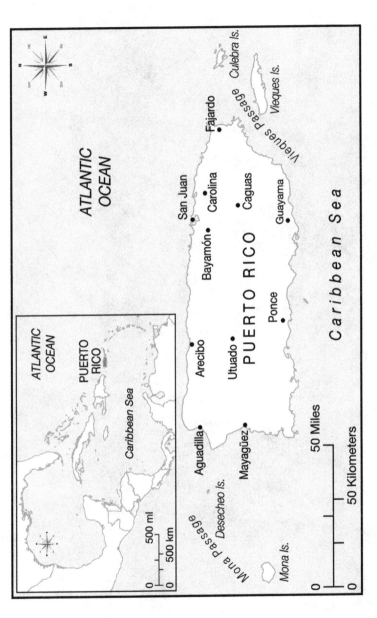

Puerto Rico in the Caribbean

PUERTO RICO

WHAT EVERYONE NEEDS TO KNOW®

INTRODUCTION
PUERTO RICO—A STATELESS
NATION

Puerto Rico has a peculiar status among Latin American and Caribbean countries. On July 25, 1898, the United States invaded the Island during the Spanish-Cuban-American War, and has since dominated the Island militarily, politically, and economically. In 1901, the US Supreme Court defined Puerto Rico as "foreign to the United States in a domestic sense" because it was neither a state of the union nor a sovereign republic. Congress granted US citizenship to all residents of Puerto Rico in 1917, but the Island remained an unincorporated territory of the United States. Puerto Rico became a US Commonwealth (or *Estado Libre Asociado*, in Spanish) in 1952, while the US federal government retained jurisdiction in most state affairs. Although Puerto Rico has a resident commissioner in the US Congress, it has no voting representatives and Puerto Ricans living on the Island cannot vote for the US president or vice president.

Today, the Island's electorate is almost evenly split between supporting Commonwealth status and becoming the 51st state of the American union; only a small minority advocates independence. US culture pervades the Island, from the influence of the English language on the Spanish vernacular to the homegrown varieties of Pentecostal churches and the proliferation of fast-food restaurants. Puerto Rico currently maintains colonial ties with the United States—as evidenced, for instance, in its dependence on massive transfer payments from the federal government and its colossal public debt to US creditors. In some respects, however, the Island does not fit the standard image of colonial societies such as the British and French overseas possessions before World War II. Contemporary Puerto Rico enjoys a greater degree of self-government than most classic colonies. The Island combines conventional elements of colonial rule with political autonomy, a relatively high standard of living (at least until recently), and a strong national culture. Puerto Rico may well be considered a "postcolonial colony" in the sense of a people with a persistent national identity but little desire for a nation-state, living in a territory that legally "belongs to but is not part of the United States."

As a US territory, Puerto Rico has been exposed to an intense penetration of US capital, commodities, laws, institutions, ideas, and customs unequaled in other Latin American countries. Yet today Puerto Ricans have a stronger sense of national identity than most Caribbean peoples, even those who enjoy political independence. Many observers have noted the growing rift between the weakened push for a sovereign government and the assertion of a vibrant culture on the Island, as manifested in language, literature, the arts, popular music, and sports, among other areas. At the beginning of the twenty-first century, Puerto Rico presents the apparent paradox of a stateless nation that has not assimilated into mainstream US culture. After 119 years of its occupation by the United States, the Island remains a Spanish-speaking, Afro-Hispanic-Caribbean nation.

In addition to its unresolved colonial dilemma, Puerto Rico is increasingly a nation on the move: a country whose porous borders are incessantly crisscrossed by migrants coming to and going away from the Island. Since the 1940s, more than two million islanders have relocated abroad. The magnitude of this exodus is even more staggering when one recalls that Puerto Rico's population was not even four million at the beginning of the twenty-first century. According to 2015 census estimates, 61.7 percent of all persons of Puerto Rican origin live in the fifty United States. At the same time, the Island has received hundreds of thousands of immigrants since the 1960s, primarily returnees and their descendants, and, secondarily, citizens of other countries, especially the Dominican Republic and Cuba. By the year 2015, 8.1 percent of the Island's residents had been born abroad, including those born in the US mainland of Puerto Rican parentage.

This combination of a prolonged exodus, together with a large influx of returnees and foreigners, makes Puerto Rico a test case of transnationalism, broadly defined as the maintenance of social, economic, and political ties across national borders. Few other countries in the Caribbean region—or even the entire world—have experienced such massive and sustained displacements of people over such a long span of time. Only nineteenth-century Ireland might serve as a historical precedent for the magnitude and persistence of the Puerto Rican diaspora. The growing diversity in the migrants' origins and destinations challenges the idea that the nation can be defined as a singular territory, birthplace, citizenship, language, culture, and identity. Above all, it is increasingly difficult to maintain that only those who were born and live on the Island, and speak Spanish, can legitimately be called Puerto Rican.

In 2006, the US Census Bureau estimated that for the first time more persons of Puerto Rican origin were living in the fifty United States than on the Island. This year also marked the onset of the Island's protracted economic recession, which propelled migration to the United States. The displacement of the Puerto Rican population reached record highs during the second decade of the twenty-first century. According to census estimates, the contemporary Puerto Rican diaspora may have surpassed the "Great Migration" between 1945 and 1965. Between 2000 and 2015, the Island's inhabitants decreased from more than 3.7 million to less than 3.5 million, largely due to high outmigration rates. The US Census Bureau estimates that the Island's population will decline to less than three million by the year 2050.

El vaivén: *moving back and forth*

The Spanish folk term for the back-and-forth movement of people between Puerto Rico and the United States is *el vaivén* (literally meaning "coming and going," or "fluctuation"). This culturally dense word alludes to the constant comings and goings in which thousands of Puerto Ricans are involved. It insinuates that some people do not stay put in one place for a long time, but move incessantly, like the wind or the waves of the sea, in response to shifting tides. Furthermore, it suggests that those who are here today may be there tomorrow, and vice versa. More ominously, *vaivén* also connotes unsteadiness, inconstancy, and oscillation. I prefer to use the term in the more neutral sense of a back-and-forth movement, without implying that people who engage in such movements never set roots in particular communities.

La nación en vaivén, the "nation on the move," might serve as an apt metaphor for the fluid and hybrid identities of Puerto Ricans on the Island and in the diaspora. This image suggests that none of the usual measures of nationhood—a shared territory, language, economy, citizenship, or sovereignty—are fixed and immutable. All of these criteria are subject to constant fluctuation and intense debate in Puerto Rico and its diaspora, even though the sense of peoplehood has proven remarkably resilient throughout.

In the past few decades, Puerto Rico has become a nation on the move through the relocation of more than half of its population to the United States and the continuing flow of people between the Island and the US mainland. Contrary to other population movements, much of the Puerto Rican exodus entails a restless movement between multiple places of origin and destination. Migration—both to and from the Island—has eroded conventional definitions of the nation as a well-bounded sovereign entity. The massive displacement of people between the Island and the US mainland since the 1940s complicates any discussion about the links among place, language, and culture. In short, contemporary Puerto Rican migration is best visualized as a pendular or "revolving-door" movement, rather than as a permanent, irrevocable, and unilateral displacement of people.

The plan of this book

Puerto Rico: What Everyone Needs to Know provides a compendium of the Island's rich history, culture, politics, and economy. In addition to this introduction, the book is divided into six chapters and an epilogue. The first chapter provides a historical overview of Puerto Rico during the Spanish colonial period (1493–1898). It focuses on how people of Native American, Spanish, and African descent settled the Island; its geopolitical role within the Spanish empire; and the gradual development of an agricultural economy, specializing in the export of coffee, sugar, and tobacco. The second chapter examines the first five decades of the US colonial regime in Puerto Rico (1898–1952), particularly its efforts to control local political and economic institutions as well as to "Americanize" the Island's culture and language. In addition, the chapter discusses how many Puerto Ricans resisted "assimilation"—culminating in majority support for political autonomy in 1952.

The third and fourth chapters of this book outline the main demographic, economic, political, and cultural features of contemporary Puerto Rico. These chapters seek to clarify the workings of the Commonwealth government and the perennial status issue—the question of what is the best form of association between Puerto Rico and the United States. The final two chapters explore the large-scale population displacement that has characterized Puerto Rico since the mid-twentieth century. In particular, they assess the multiple demographic,

economic, political, and cultural repercussions of the continuing exodus of Puerto Ricans to the United States.

A biographical note

I was born in Havana, Cuba, but was raised in Panama and
Puerto Rico. My parents decided to leave Cuba after the
Revolution in 1960, when I was only three years old. The
family first settled in Panama, then moved to Puerto Rico in
1966. I spent most of my childhood and adolescence in the
San Juan metropolitan area, mainly in the growing suburb of
Bayamón. Upon graduating from high school, I completed my
university studies in the United States and then returned to
live and work on the Island, where I married and raised my
own family. I was a professor and academic administrator at
the University of the Sacred Heart in Santurce (1985–94) and
at the University of Puerto Rico in Río Piedras (1994–2012).
In 2012, I accepted an administrative and teaching position at
Florida International University in Miami. Like many residents
of Puerto Rico, I was compelled to leave the Island searching
for better professional opportunities amid a profound economic crisis. Since resettling in Miami, I have kept abreast of
Puerto Rican affairs by reading the Island's daily newspapers
online, traveling frequently to San Juan, conducting research,
participating in academic conferences, and reviewing recent
scholarly works about Puerto Rico and its diaspora.

Since I was very young, I was troubled by the constant
question, "where are you from?" I usually answered, "I was
born in Cuba, but I grew up in Puerto Rico." Half in jest, I often
declare that I am Cuba-Rican, rather than Cuban American,
because until recently I had never lived continuously for long
periods of time in the United States, even though I have been
a US citizen since 1985. My Cuban birth, coupled with long-
time residence in Puerto Rico, gives me an odd status somewhere in between stranger and near-native of the Island.
My personal diasporic condition has undoubtedly shaped

my research agenda, especially on transnational migration from the Hispanic Caribbean, mainly in Puerto Rico, Cuba, and the Dominican Republic. Despite the shifting terminology and objects of study, I have been primarily interested in how cross-border movements impact people's sense of who they are and where they belong. Much of this book is informed by this overriding concern—perhaps an intellectual obsession—with national and transnational identities. I dedicate this work to all those who, like myself, have recently moved from the Island to Florida looking for a better life.

1

PUERTO RICO BEFORE 1898

What groups inhabited Puerto Rico before the Spanish Conquest?

The Taínos were the first indigenous inhabitants of the Americas to come into contact with Europeans. They occupied much of the Larger Antilles, including what is now Puerto Rico, which they called Borinquen or Borikén, when Christopher Columbus and his Spanish caravels arrived there on November 19, 1493. (Columbus named the island San Juan Bautista in honor of St. John the Baptist.) The term Taíno means "good" or "noble" in the Arawak language, and indeed Taíno culture has traditionally been romanticized as the prototype of "the noble savage." The word *boricua* is now used as a synonym for Puerto Rican, often implying a strong emotional attachment to the Island and its culture.

Archaeologists have documented that the ancestors of the Taínos—the so-called Salaloid people—started to migrate around 500 BC to the Caribbean islands from the Amazon Basin of South America, along the Orinoco River near present-day Venezuela and Guyana. Linguists have shown that the now-extinct language spoken by the Taínos was a dialect of the Arawak language. Others have speculated about their historical origins in Mesoamerica, especially the Yucatán peninsula of contemporary Mexico. In any case, the Taíno people flourished in Borinquen for approximately five centuries before the Spaniards' arrival. At the time, Puerto Rico functioned as a natural frontier between the Taínos of the Larger Antilles and the so-called Caribs of the Lesser Antilles.

By the late fifteenth century, the Taínos had settled in relatively dense and permanent villages (*yucayeques*) of between one thousand and five thousand people, each governed by a chief or *cacique*. These chiefdoms represented an intermediate level of political centralization between tribes and states. They were organized into regional chiefdoms, each headed by the most prominent *cacique* (during the early sixteenth century, forty-four such regional chiefdoms existed in Puerto Rico). Many local places on the Island still bear the indigenous names of *caciques*, such as the municipalities of Caguas, Mayagüez, Humacao, and Loíza.

The Taínos developed a system of extensive agriculture, based on the planting of cassava (yucca), sweet potato, corn, and other root crops in small mounds (*conucos*). They practiced a farming technique now known as slash-and-burn, consisting of clearing the trees and bushes in a plot of land, allowing it to dry, and then planting various types of crops. The land lay fallow after the soil was exhausted and was reused at a later time. This system of cultivation met the food demands of a growing population.

The Taínos worshipped multiple deities, known as *cemíes*, which they sculpted in stone, wood, shells, and other materials as anthropomorphic figures representing the major forces of nature, such as rain and hurricanes. The Taínos built large ceremonial courts (*bateyes*) to pay homage to their gods, perform dances called *areítos*, and play ball games. A common ritual was the *cohiba* or *cohoba*, whereby the witch healer or shaman (*behique*) inhaled the smoke of tobacco leaves, entered into a trance, and divined the future. The *behique* also prescribed the use of medicinal plants for various types of illnesses.

The kinship system of the Taínos was matrilineal and polygynous, meaning that they traced their lineage through the mother's side of the family and that men could marry many women. The rank of *cacique* was transmitted to his sister's sons. Aside from the *caciques*, Taíno society was internally divided into three major groups: the *nitaínos* (nobles), *behiques*, and *naborías* (laborers or servants). The Spanish conquistadors interpreted these strata as social classes, but the socioeconomic differences among them were not as large and institutionalized as in capitalist societies.

Why did the indigenous population of Puerto Rico decline so quickly after Spanish colonization?

Spanish colonists and African slaves quickly replaced the Taíno population, roughly between 1493 and 1550. The exact number of the indigenous inhabitants of Borinquen is still disputed. Estimates have ranged widely between 16,000 and 600,000 people before the conquistadors' arrival. The best documented sources suggest that the pre-Columbian population probably numbered about 100,000. The first official count by the Spaniards in 1511 found approximately 5,500 enslaved Indians. Twenty years later, only 1,545 Indians (including 1,041 enslaved ones) were counted on the Island. The last time the Spanish census of the Island included "Indians" as a separate category, in 1802, it found 2,300 persons, all in the jurisdiction of San Germán.

The Spanish Conquest of Puerto Rico and the Caribbean unleashed one of the greatest demographic catastrophes of the modern world, which some have dubbed a genocide. War, slavery, disease, intermarriage, suicide, and migration to other territories decimated the indigenous population of the Greater Antilles during the first half of the sixteenth century. Violent confrontations with Spanish soldiers took a heavy toll on the Taínos. Furthermore, native workers toiled in slave-like conditions under the *encomienda*, a system of forced labor that "entrusted" native workers to Spanish colonists. The widespread mistreatment of indigenous workers, especially in the exploitation of the gold mines, debilitated the local population and resulted in a high death rate.

Moreover, contagious illnesses brought from Europe devastated the population of the Larger Antilles, especially Hispaniola, Puerto Rico, and Cuba. Because of their previous isolation, the indigenous inhabitants had no biological immunity to these imported diseases. The most common epidemics were smallpox, measles, the bubonic plague, dysentery, influenza, and typhus. In addition, the indigenous population suffered malnutrition due to the destruction of local crops by war and frequent hurricanes. Finally, many Taínos sought refuge in the inner mountains, far from Spanish settlements, or fled to neighboring islands, particularly the Lesser Antilles, which were neglected by Spanish colonization.

Persons claiming Taíno ancestry have survived in Puerto Rico as well as in other Caribbean countries, such as the Dominican Republic and Cuba. The Spanish Conquest did not totally annihilate the Taínos; many of them intermingled with Spanish settlers and African slaves. Today, many people believe they can trace their lineages to the pre-Columbian population of the region. Genetic studies have found that about two-thirds of the contemporary Puerto Rican population descend from Native Americans, mainly through the maternal side of the family. A Taíno revival movement has gained strength since the 1980s, especially among Puerto Ricans in New York and New Jersey. The Taíno Inter-Tribal Council was founded in New Jersey in 1993 and operated until 2001. The United Confederation of Taíno People, established in New York in 1998, listed eight affiliated organizations in the US mainland. Although small in number, these self-described Taínos have sought to reconstruct and preserve their ancestors' language, culture, and religion.

Who was Agüeybaná II?

Agüeybaná II, also known as the Brave (ca. 1470–1511), was one of the most powerful Taíno chiefs of Borinquen, particularly in the southwest coast of the Island, at the time of the arrival of the Spanish conquistadors. Following local customs, he inherited his position from Agüeybaná I (the Elder), his maternal uncle, upon the latter's death in 1510. The name Agüeybaná means "Great Sun" in the Taíno language. According to traditional accounts, Agüeybaná II ordered the drowning of a Spanish soldier, Diego Salcedo, to prove that the conquistadors were not immortal deities.

In 1511, Agüeybaná II led an indigenous rebellion against the Spanish colonizers, burning down the town of Sotomayor (present-day Aguada) and executing the main *encomendero*, Cristóbal de Sotomayor, and about 80 other Spaniards. In retaliation, the Spanish governor, Juan Ponce de León, led a military force to pacify the Island, killing Agüeybaná II and many of his followers at the Battle of Yagüecas in 1511. After his death, Agüeybaná II became a literary inspiration for Spanish and Puerto Rican writers from the sixteenth century until well into the twenty-first century. Many authors have depicted him as an icon of native resistance against Spanish colonialism on the Island.

Who was Juan Ponce de León?

Ponce de León (1460–1521) was a Spanish conquistador, soldier, and explorer. Born into a noble family in the northern province of present-day Valladolid, Spain, he probably traveled with Christopher Columbus on his second voyage to the Americas (1493–96). He was appointed governor of the eastern province of Higüey in Hispaniola in 1504, as a reward for helping to suppress an indigenous uprising led by the *cacique* Cotubanamá the year before. The Spanish governor of Hispaniola authorized Ponce de León to explore the nearby island of Puerto Rico (then called San Juan Bautista) in 1508. That same year he founded the earliest Spanish settlement (Caparra) on the north coast of Puerto Rico. Ponce de León became the first Spanish governor of Puerto Rico in 1510. He and other conquistadors forced the Taínos to work in the gold mines, construct fortifications, and grow crops. Ponce de León had to surrender the governorship of Puerto Rico and was replaced by Columbus's son, Diego, in 1511.

In 1513, Ponce de León organized a colonizing expedition to what is now Florida, which he named (after Easter season or *Pascua Florida*) and claimed for the Spanish Crown. He landed on the northeast coast of the peninsula, probably near present-day Saint Augustine, searching for the legendary island of Bimini (and less likely the Fountain of Youth). After spending some time in Puerto Rico and later in Spain, he returned to Florida in 1521 and attempted to found a settlement on the southwest coast, which was later abandoned. During a battle with the Calusa tribe, he was wounded with a poisoned arrow and eventually died after sailing to Havana, Cuba. Ponce de León's remains are buried in the Cathedral of San Juan, and the Island's fourth largest city, Ponce, is named after him.

What was the impact of African slavery in Puerto Rico?

As the Island's indigenous inhabitants dwindled during the early sixteenth century, the Spanish Crown turned to the importation of African slaves. The crown first granted permission to introduce African slaves to the Americas as early as 1501, and several hundred were brought to Puerto Rico over the next few decades. By 1530, the first Spanish census of the Island counted 2,284 black slaves, more than half (54.7 percent) of a total population of 4,170. Throughout the sixteenth century, approximately 7,000 African slaves were legally imported to the Island, while others were brought through contraband. They worked in the gold mines and sugar cane fields, planted ginger, prepared hides, produced food, built forts and churches, and provided domestic service. African slaves became the backbone of the sugar industry in Puerto Rico and the rest of the Caribbean. They tended to settle in the Island's coastal plains, near towns such as Ponce, Mayagüez, and Guayama, where sugar plantations concentrated.

Despite the continuous influx of slaves, the population of African origin never reached the high proportions found in other Caribbean colonies such as Cuba or Haiti (St. Domingue). Between 54,000 and 75,000 slaves were introduced to Puerto Rico from 1509 to 1860. According to the first official census in 1765, the Island's inhabitants comprised 44,833 persons, of whom 5,037 were slaves (11.2 percent of the population). The number of slaves, both black and mulatto, grew quickly to 18,053 in 1795 (13.9 percent of the total). The greatest number of African slaves—perhaps 60,000 or 80 percent of the total—arrived between 1800 and 1865. Puerto Rico's slave population grew from 13,333 in 1802 to a high of 51,265 in 1846. By then, slaves composed 11.6 percent of the Island's population. The decline in the number of slaves was primarily due to their growing cost. On the eve of emancipation in 1873, less than 2 percent (29,335) of Puerto Rico's inhabitants were enslaved.

Unfortunately, it is difficult to specify the ethnic origins of African slaves imported to Puerto Rico. From the sixteenth century on, most slaves came from the coastal region of West Africa, especially from the Senegal River to the Gulf of Guinea, although many also came from the interior of the African continent, including the Congo and Angola. The Yoruba, Congo, Mandinga, Calabar, Wolof, and other groups influenced the development of Afro-Puerto Rican culture. Their substantial contribution to language, music, dance, religion, art, and cuisine is still evident in contemporary Puerto Rico.

One of the unintended demographic consequences of African slavery in Puerto Rico was the emergence of a large "free colored" population, composed of the offspring of African, Indian, and Spanish people. This population constituted a disenfranchised "caste" within Spanish colonial society, legally set apart from whites, Indians, and slaves. The free people of color were in turn subdivided into two main racial categories: *pardos* (light-skinned mulattos) and *morenos* (dark-skinned mulattos and blacks). By 1790, free people of color (40.2 percent) nearly equaled whites (43.3 percent) as the leading sector of Puerto Rico's population (12.3 percent were slaves). The free colored group continued to grow during the nineteenth century as one of the main sources of the Island's racially mixed inhabitants.

What was the role of immigration in shaping Puerto Rico's population?

As in other Caribbean countries, the present-day population of Puerto Rico is basically the result of immigration. The Island's inhabitants during the Spanish colonial period (1493–1898) drew on two major sources: Spanish immigrants and African slaves. Early Spanish immigrants were mostly men from Andalusia, Extremadura, and other southern regions of Spain. Many of them mated with women of indigenous and African ancestry, thus giving rise to the first *mestizos* and mulattoes on the Island.

Puerto Rico's population grew at a slow pace between the sixteenth and eighteenth centuries. Since the mid-eighteenth century, thousands of soldiers, sailors, convict laborers, stowaways, deportees, deserters, and runaway slaves resettled on the Island. In the late eighteenth century, population growth accelerated. After the Haitian Revolution (1791–1804), numerous French and Spanish subjects, displaced from Hispaniola and Louisiana, took refuge in Puerto Rico. Another wave of refugees arrived between 1810 and 1830, fleeing the independence wars in Venezuela. After 1815, the expansion of sugar and coffee plantations attracted an increasing flow of immigrants, largely from peninsular Spain, the Canary Islands, and Majorca, but also from Corsica and other parts of Europe, South America, the Caribbean, as well as greater numbers of slaves from Africa.

What was life like in Puerto Rico under Spanish rule?

During the early sixteenth century, the Spanish Crown transplanted the most significant political, military, economic, and religious institutions of the Iberian Peninsula to the Americas. Under the theory of European mercantilism prevalent at the time, the accumulation of gold, silver, and other precious metals largely drove the expansion of the Spanish empire, which privileged the mineral-rich colonies of Mexico and Peru. The empire was initially subdivided into two viceroyalties—New Spain (1535) and Peru (1543)—to which the viceroyalties of New Granada (1717) and the River Plate (1776) were later added. The viceroyalty of New Spain covered Mexico, much of Central America, and the Caribbean, including Puerto Rico.

For most of the Spanish colonial period, the maximum authority in Puerto Rico was the governor, who also held the title of captain general, and was appointed by the Spanish Crown. Between 1564 and 1898 (except for a brief interruption between 1822 and 1823), the governor of Puerto Rico was a military man. The concentration of both civil and military power in one person completely militarized the Island's political system. Since 1693, the governor appointed a personal representative in each of the main towns—called a war lieutenant (*teniente a guerra*). Each municipal settlement had its own *cabildo* or town council, which represented local interests within the colonial administration. Except for a short period of democratization in the early 1800s, the entire colonial system was highly centralized, hierarchical, and monarchical.

Between 1584 and 1809, the government of Puerto Rico depended financially on the Mexican *situado*, a regular subsidy from the viceroyalty of New Spain. Most of the funds were used to maintain a permanent garrison in San Juan, which had become a key site for the defense of Spain's continental territories in the Americas. During the second half of the eighteenth century, the Bourbon kings of Spain sought to make Puerto Rico more profitable and implemented administrative and economic reforms as part of broader institutional changes within the empire. After the visit of Field Marshal Alejandro O'Reilly (1722–94) in 1765, the Island experienced modest economic growth, mainly through the expansion of cash crops such as sugar, coffee, tobacco, and cotton. However, Spanish colonial policy prevented the development of local manufacturing industries (such as textile production) that might compete with those of the metropole.

What was the Island's primary role within the Spanish empire?

The Island's first Spanish governor, Ponce de León, established a small settlement in Caparra in 1508, but reluctantly transferred the city in 1521 to its present site across the bay, because of its better access to the harbor, soil and vegetation, and defensive potential. Given the Island's strategic position within the Spanish Antilles, the city was repeatedly attacked by Indian groups from neighboring Caribbean islands, as well as by Spain's European rivals, especially Britain, France, and the Netherlands. In response, Spanish authorities began the construction of La Fortaleza (the Fortress) in 1532 and a second fort, San Felipe del Morro, in 1539 at the main entrance to the San Juan bay. Smaller citadels such as San Cristóbal were built to defend the city against land-based attacks, and El Cañuelo, in Isla de Cabras, to protect the western entrance to the harbor.

Since 1529, Spanish authorities dubbed Puerto Rico "the key to the Indies" because of its location at one of the main entrances to the Caribbean Sea. San Juan, in particular, played a largely defensive role within the Spanish empire from the mid-sixteenth century to the late eighteenth century. After the exhaustion of the Island's gold mines and the decimation of the indigenous population (1493–1550), Puerto Rico was marginalized from the primary trade routes between the mainland colonies of the Americas, especially Mexico and Peru, and the Iberian Peninsula. Between 1561 and 1776, the Spanish *flota* (fleet) system organized two convoys of ships between

Seville and, later, Cádiz in Spain and Veracruz, Portobelo, and Cartagena in the Caribbean area, before making a rendezvous in Havana and continuing on to Spain.

Preserving control over Puerto Rico was crucial to Spanish military strategy in the Caribbean. Therefore, the capital city became a military bastion, as well as the administrative and religious seat of the Spanish colonial regime on the Island. The Spanish armed forces closely regulated the use of spaces within the elaborate defensive system that surrounded the city. Accordingly, military authorities did not allow the areas located near the fortifications to be employed for residential development, commercial establishments, leisure activities, or other civic purposes. Thus, San Juan remained a modestly sized urban center for centuries.

Between 1631 and 1641, San Juan became a completely walled city, dominated by two imposing fortresses, San Felipe del Morro and San Cristóbal, which ensured Spanish control of Puerto Rico until 1898. These military structures, initiated in the sixteenth century and completed in the eighteenth, transformed the natural landscape of San Juan and converted it into one of the most garrisoned cities in the New World. The fortifications around the capital city contributed to a growing gulf between the colonial administration and most of the local population, scattered throughout the Island. Now considered a world heritage site and a major tourist destination, El Morro Castle has become one of the most recognizable icons of the city and the Island as a whole. As the governor's official residence, La Fortaleza is the oldest executive mansion in continuous use in the Americas.

How did the Catholic Church shape Puerto Rican culture?

From the beginning until the end of Spanish colonization, Catholicism was the official religion of Puerto Rico. In 1511, Pope Julius II established the Archdiocese of San Juan as one of the first three ecclesiastical provinces of the Catholic Church in the Americas, after Santo Domingo and Concepción de la Vega in Hispaniola. The Spanish State and the Catholic Church were practically fused into one. In particular, the Catholic Church monopolized education on the Island until 1898. Only in 1869—during a short period of liberal reform in Spain—was freedom of religion tolerated in Puerto Rico. That same year, the first Anglican congregation was authorized in Ponce, and a year later a group of West Indian immigrants received permission to establish an Anglican school in Vieques. Nonetheless, the Catholic hierarchy continued to view other religions as threats to its exclusive status on the Island.

Spanish missionary priests sought to "save souls" by imposing their religious beliefs and customs on the indigenous inhabitants and later African slaves. To this end, they brought countless Catholic institutions, rituals, and dogmas to the New World. The Catholic Church profoundly structured the everyday life of Puerto Ricans through the annual calendar of Catholic saints and other ritual celebrations, such as Christmas and Easter, as well as customs related to the sacrament of Baptism and the devotion to the Virgin Mary. Major civic events such as royal weddings and births were celebrated in Puerto Rico with religious pomp and solemnity. Singing, dancing, games, and sometimes horseracing accompanied religious festivities. The secular influence of the Church was visible in the layout of colonial cities and towns, which invariably had a central plaza with the *ayuntamiento* (town hall) located on one side and the Catholic church on the other. The names of numerous municipalities, streets, plazas, and forts still evoke the Catholic faith. Children were often baptized after the saint whose feast day coincided with their birthdate. A Catholic worldview permeated Puerto Rican culture through folk beliefs, customs, icons, prayers, and devotions.

However, the process of evangelization was partial and superficial in ample sectors of the population, especially among the peasantry in the most remote areas of the Island. The insufficient number of parishes and priests, as well as the concentration of Church resources in urban areas, distanced most ordinary citizens from orthodox Catholicism. Many Puerto Ricans filled the void left by a formal liturgy and sacramental life with objects of devotion such as household altars, sung rosaries, and engravings of the saints. The cult of the saints was the core of popular religiosity, and each town had its own patron saint, especially the various apparitions of the Virgin Mary.

Nowadays, most Puerto Ricans still identify themselves as Catholic and practice a popular form of religiosity derived from Mediterranean Catholicism, particularly from rural Spain. Many follow Catholic customs such as frequently invoking the name of God, the Virgin, and the saints in ordinary conversation, treating godparents as part of the family, and wearing medals, crucifixes, and other religious symbols. Less common practices today include following the Church's teachings on birth control, divorce, and attending Mass and other major ritual observances.

How did the folk art of sculpting the saints develop in Puerto Rico?

Santos is the Spanish name for sacred images of the Catholic saints, the Virgin Mary, the Magi, Christ, and other religious characters and episodes from the Bible and Catholic folklore. These images were usually carved in wood and then decorated with paint, metal, and precious stones. Santos tended to be small—typically fewer than twelve inches high—because they had to fit within a humble niche. They were commonly found in Catholic churches and household altars throughout Spain and Latin America. Santos were widespread in Puerto Rico, especially in rural areas with limited access to clergy and temples.

The earliest surviving examples of santos were probably brought to Puerto Rico from Spain and other European countries, such as Italy and France, during the sixteenth century.

The first known Puerto Rican–made *santos* imitated the baroque style prevalent in Spain at the end of the eighteenth century. Like their Spanish prototypes, these images sought to reproduce as realistically as possible the human body, the landscape, and other aspects of the physical environment. The oldest Puerto Rican *santos* resembled those from Spain, Mexico, Guatemala, and Santo Domingo during most of the Spanish colonial period.

Roughly between 1750 and 1898, Puerto Rican *santos* developed a distinctive style. The images gradually lost their natural appearance, while their posture adopted a frontal, rigid stance, either sitting or standing. Their anatomical proportions were deliberately deformed to stress their supernatural character. Traditional costumes were often abandoned; facial expressions were softened; and new characters and scenes were portrayed. Puerto Rican *santeros* increasingly represented local devotions such as the Miracle of the Virgin of Hormigueros, the Three Kings and the Three Maries, and the Lonely Soul. By far the most venerated figure during the Spanish colonial period was the Virgin of Monserrate, transplanted from Catalonia but transformed into a black or mulatto woman. Other favorite subjects were the Three Kings, the various apparitions of the Virgin (especially at Candlemas and Bethlehem), Saint Anthony of Padua, the Nativity, and the Crucifixion.

Puerto Rican *santos* proliferated during the nineteenth century to satisfy a growing demand for objects of worship, particularly in the most isolated peasant areas. The art of sculpting saints was especially popular in the inner highlands, along the central mountain range. There, subsistence farmers of mixed Spanish, African, and indigenous origins developed a folk version of Catholicism centered on the cult of the saints in domestic shrines. During the second half of the twentieth century, *santos* became one of the most significant icons of Puerto Rico's national identity. Most traditional *santos* are now held in private collections, galleries, and museums, and have become objects of commercial consumption and speculation, especially by art collectors and tourists.

Who was José Campeche?

José Campeche (1751–1809) was one of the leading Latin American painters of the eighteenth century. He was born in San Juan to a black father, who had purchased his freedom through his savings as a master woodcarver, and a white immigrant mother from the Canary Islands. The young Campeche was a largely self-taught artist who copied engravings and illustrations from Europe, mainly from Spain. He later became an apprentice under the Spanish painter Luis Paret y Alcázar (1746–99), who was exiled in San Juan for two years (1775–78) and taught Campeche to cultivate rococo motifs, a style originating in eighteenth-century France and characterized by detailed ornamentation.

Campeche's extensive artwork—comprising between four hundred and five hundred oil and watercolor paintings—focused on religious images and portraits. His most abundant production consisted of images of the Catholic saints, Jesus Christ, and the Virgin Mary (particularly the Virgin of Bethlehem and Carmel), usually commissioned to decorate church altars, especially in the Cathedral of San Juan. Campeche is now best known for his realistic depictions of prominent figures of his time in San Juan, including several governors, bishops, and state officials. Among them stand out a series of five portraits of *Ladies on Horseback* (ca. 1785) and another of Governor Miguel Antonio de Ustáriz (1792).

Although Campeche did not feature many ordinary people and scenes of everyday life in his paintings, he documented the most significant events, personalities, and devotions of his time. Campeche's artwork can now be seen in museums, churches, and private collections in Puerto Rico, Venezuela, and the United States. In 2011, the Institute of Puerto Rican Culture initiated a public cultural event in his memory,

La Campechada, in the historic district of San Juan, where he was born and is buried, in the Church of Saint Joseph. The annual event gathers hundreds of artists, artisans, performers, dancers, and others interested in celebrating Campeche's artistic legacy in Puerto Rico.

How did immigrants contribute to the expansion of the Island's agricultural economy after 1815?

The military, administrative, and economic restructuring of the Spanish empire under the Bourbon dynasty (1700–1808) gave greater prominence to the Atlantic lowlands of the Americas, particularly in the Caribbean. By 1825 Cuba and Puerto Rico were Spain's last remaining colonies in the New World, and were integrated into the international market for tropical commodities, especially sugar, coffee, and tobacco. Puerto Rico was transformed from a neglected military outpost depending on subsistence agriculture, cattle ranching, and contraband trade into a prosperous agricultural colony. In particular, the volume of sugar exports multiplied threefold, from 291,892 *quintales* (one *quintal* is equivalent to one hundred pounds) in 1828–32 to 1,052,437 *quintales* in 1848–52. By 1870, the Island produced about 7 percent of the world's sugar and had become the second largest exporter of sugar in the Western hemisphere, after Cuba.

Since the early nineteenth century, Spanish colonial authorities sought to stimulate Puerto Rico's agricultural and commercial development. One of the main public policies was to attract a large number of immigrants with capital and skills. In 1815, the Spanish Crown issued a royal decree (*Cédula de Gracias*) encouraging the entry of Europeans from friendly countries who practiced the Catholic faith. Among other incentives, the decree granted land and allowed for the importation of slaves and machinery, free of taxes, to those foreigners who met the requirements established by King Ferdinand VII. More than six thousand household heads took advantage of these opportunities during the first three decades of the nineteenth century. As originally planned, foreign immigration contributed substantially to large-scale commercial agriculture—particularly sugar cultivation—on the Island.

Between 1800 and 1850, one-third of all free immigrants in Puerto Rico were "people of color," including both "mulattos" and "blacks" (*pardos, morenos*, and *negros*, in the terminology of the period). Most came from other Caribbean islands, mainly St. Domingue (Haiti), Curaçao, St. Thomas, Martinique, and St. Croix. Many were skilled workers, including carpenters, masons, and blacksmiths. Others were farmers, sellers, and domestics. These immigrants contributed to the growth of the free colored population on the Island.

Thousands of Europeans, especially from Spain and other Mediterranean countries, also moved to Puerto Rico during the nineteenth century. The majority came from the Iberian Peninsula, the Canary Islands, and the Balearic Islands. Officially sponsored by the Spanish Crown since the late seventeenth century, the large-scale influx of Canary Islanders extended throughout the nineteenth century. *Canarios* would play a leading role in the foundation of towns, the emergence of a Creole dialect of Spanish, and in numerous rural customs in Puerto Rico, such as the devotion to the Virgin of Candlemas, cockfights, and country music. Other ethnic groups from the peripheral regions of Spain would arrive later, including Catalans, Majorcans, Basques, Asturians, and Galicians.

A significant minority of nineteenth-century immigrants came from more than a dozen different countries, among them France, Italy, Santo Domingo, and Venezuela. Most numerous were the French, who concentrated in the western zone of the Island, particularly in Mayagüez. Among French subjects, Corsicans stood out and were closely tied to the coffee industry, especially in the southern and western regions of the Island, congregating in towns such as Yauco, San Germán, and Lares. Italians were the second largest group of Europeans, who settled mainly in coastal cities like San Juan, Ponce, and Mayagüez.

How did the intensive cultivation of sugar and coffee transform the Island's physical and cultural landscape?

The settlement patterns of sugar plantations and coffee *haciendas* differed considerably. *Haciendas* consisted of isolated peasant households surrounded by a few acres of cultivated land. In contrast, plantations were characterized by nucleated villages of wage laborers, along with slave barracks in the main property. Meanwhile, smallholder areas, growing tobacco and minor crops, were intermediate in size between the clustered plantation villages and the scattered *hacienda* communities. These differing environments shaped the practices and mentalities of agricultural workers in Puerto Rico. Not surprisingly, the coastal lowlands and inner highlands developed distinct subcultures that persisted well into the twentieth century.

A large mass of free but economically underprivileged farmers of European and mixed ancestry were the primary colonizers of the inner highlands. Here they led an isolated and independent way of life based on subsistence agriculture and cattle raising from the sixteenth to the eighteenth centuries. This was the land of the *jíbaro*—the rustic, seminomadic peasant—idealized by modern Puerto Ricans in many nostalgic writings and submitted to the status of debt peonage in the coffee *haciendas* that dominated the mountain economy after 1850. Many of these landless farmers were forced to work as day laborers (*jornaleros*) during the infamous regime of the *libreta* (day laborer's passbook), instituted by Governor Juan de la Pezuela in 1849 and lasting until 1873.

Jíbaros, peons, and *agregados* (sharecroppers) were preindustrial rural types who cultivated coffee, tobacco, and other minor crops on small plots of land in groups of families and with their hired hands. One of the main ethnic antecedents of this peasantry were immigrants from the Canary Islands, who came in large numbers to Puerto Rico in the eighteenth and nineteenth centuries. *Canarios* and their Creole descendants founded many of the small towns of the interior and the tobacco-growing municipalities near the coast. The Spanish spoken in contemporary Puerto Rico shares many elements with the Spanish of the Canary Islands.

A different type of agricultural enterprise took shape on the coastal plains: the sugar plantation. This system of production required an abundant labor force for the cutting and manufacturing of sugarcane, and enslaved Africans were imported to fill this demand. Slaves were concentrated around the major urban centers that were the capitals of plantation agriculture: San Juan, Ponce, Mayagüez, Arecibo, and Guayama. The nature of the landscape (sugarcane is better suited to lowland plain areas) and access to export ports determined their coastal location. To this day, the two most "African" towns in Puerto Rico remain Loíza Aldea, a predominantly black community on the northern shore east of San Juan, and Guayama, "the city of the witches," as it is commonly known, on the southern coast near Ponce. It was primarily in the lowlands that an Afro-Puerto Rican subculture evolved among plantation workers.

What was the role of coffee agriculture in Puerto Rico in the second half of the nineteenth century?

Coffee became Puerto Rico's leading export crop between the 1870s and 1890s, primarily as a result of growing demand and rising prices for coffee in European markets such as Spain, France, and Germany. Consequently, the Island's coffee-growing municipalities—including Utuado, Jayuya, Lares, Yauco, Adjuntas, and San Sebastián del Pepino—experienced rapid economic and population growth. Before the coffee boom, the main economic activities in Utuado and other neighboring areas had been cattle raising and subsistence agriculture. Many residents also participated in contraband trade, selling animals and food in exchange for textiles and tools from foreign merchants.

Much of Puerto Rican literature and history has mythologized the nineteenth-century coffee *hacienda* as the "golden age" for the rise of a Creole identity, with the *jíbaro* embodying that identity. However, the actual circumstances of the Island's coffee boom during the second half of the nineteenth century were anything but romantic. By the 1890s, land was increasingly concentrated in large estates that displaced small and medium landowners. Countless subsistence farmers were forced to work for a wage or as sharecroppers (*agregados*) in those agricultural enterprises. Because most *haciendas* owners could not afford to purchase a large number of slaves, they relied substantially on the coerced labor of *jornaleros*. Working and living conditions for most rural workers deteriorated, as reflected in their daily diet, as coffee replaced subsistence crops like plantain, corn, rice, and sweet potatoes. The expansion of coffee cultivation also entailed the destruction of timber-yielding forests, sparing only trees (like plantain and banana) that provided the necessary shade to coffee plants.

How did the Island's population grow during the Spanish colonial period?

For most of its history, the vast majority of the Island's inhabitants resided in small farms and isolated towns. Until the nineteenth century, most Puerto Ricans lived in small and simple *bohíos*, reminiscent of indigenous thatched huts. Toward the end of the seventeenth century, Puerto Rico had only two major urban centers: San Juan on the northeast coast and San Germán in the southwest. Both were small in size and modest in style, except for their military and religious buildings. Much of the Island's central mountainous region remained uninhabited until the second half of the nineteenth century.

The Island's physical features largely determined the geographic distribution of the population during the first three centuries of Spanish colonization. The coastal plains were much more amenable to settlement than the rugged interior. Until the end of the eighteenth century, most of Puerto Rico's inhabitants concentrated on the northwest coast, while the mountainous region attracted few settlers. The most important economic activities—cattle raising and commercial agriculture—were carried out in the northern lowlands. During the first half of the nineteenth century, the expansion of sugar plantations on the coastal plains expelled many inhabitants toward the central mountain range.

The western highlands developed in response to the consolidation of coffee agriculture during the second half of the nineteenth century. By the end of the century, the most rapid population growth occurred in coffee-growing areas like Utuado, Yauco, Lares, and Maricao. Between 1887 and 1899, the interior municipalities grew by 22.2 percent, compared to 17.6 percent for the coastal municipalities. Altogether, thirty-four towns were founded throughout the nineteenth century, mainly in the Island's inner highlands.

Puerto Rico had already become a densely settled country in the late nineteenth century, although most of its residents were dispersed throughout the countryside. By 1899, Puerto Rico's inhabitants reached nearly a million (940,353), with 277 people per square mile (compared to 36 in Cuba). Population density was higher in the western and northern regions of the Island than in the southern and eastern regions. The first US census of the Island in 1899 confirmed the predominantly rural character of the population. In that year, 78.6 percent of the population lived in places with fewer than 1,000 persons. Only two cities had more than 25,000 residents: San Juan and Ponce.

Why did Puerto Rico not become independent from Spain?

Contrary to the mainland Spanish American colonies, Puerto Rico did not develop a vigorous pro-independence movement during the first three decades of the nineteenth century. The

Spanish colonial government quickly dismantled a few isolated attempts to separate the Island from its metropole. While
most of Spain's possessions from Mexico to Argentina rebelled
against colonial rule, Puerto Rico (and Cuba) remained loyal
to the Spanish Crown until the end of the nineteenth century.
During this period, the prevailing political current in Puerto
Rico was a reformist, liberal, and autonomist ideology that
sought limited self-government within the Spanish colonial regime. Puerto Rican separatists were a radical minority
within the Creole elite, especially among professionals and
intellectuals. Furthermore, many members of the upper class
were conservatives (known as *incondicionales*) who supported
Spain's absolutist monarchy.

Several factors help explain the weakness of the pro-
independence movement in Puerto Rico throughout the nineteenth century. To begin, Puerto Rico was home to a relatively
large core of Spanish military, civilian, and religious officials,
together with merchants and landowners linked to the colonial administration. Thousands of Spanish troops were stationed in San Juan, especially after their defeat in the mainland
colonies of Spanish America after 1810. Indeed, Puerto Rico
was a focus of Spanish military operations against Venezuelan
insurgents in 1810–11.

Second, Spanish authorities systematically persecuted,
imprisoned, executed, or expelled the leaders of any groups
suspected of plotting against the colonial regime. For most of
the nineteenth century, the main separatist leaders were exiled
in the United States, Latin America, or Europe. Third, thousands of Spanish loyalists from former Spanish territories like
Venezuela and Louisiana and conservative French refugees
from St. Domingue (later Haiti) resettled in Puerto Rico during
the first quarter of the nineteenth century. Fourth, many members of the Creole elite, themselves descendants of Spaniards,
felt attached to the "Mother Country" and some feared a slave
uprising should Puerto Rico become self-governing. Finally,
the pro-independence movement lacked a clear socioeconomic

project to improve the living conditions of the local population. The isolation, dispersal, poverty, and illiteracy of most of the Island's inhabitants contributed to a feeble opposition against Spanish rule.

What was the Lares uprising and why did it fail?

The Lares revolt (or *Grito de Lares*, in Spanish) was the most significant armed insurrection aimed at wresting independence from Spain and creating a sovereign republic in Puerto Rico. Organized by the exiled physician Ramón Emeterio Betances, the rebellion was originally planned for the town of Camuy beginning on September 29, 1868, but was moved to Lares on September 23 because Spanish colonial authorities had discovered the conspiracy. The authorities prevented Betances and an expeditionary force of three thousand men from reaching Puerto Rico from nearby St. Thomas.

On the evening of September 23, about four hundred insurgents, led by a Venezuelan-born local landowner, Manuel Rojas (1831–1903), took the town of Lares in the west-central highlands of Puerto Rico. Chanting ¡*Viva Puerto Rico libre!* ("Long live free Puerto Rico!"), they proclaimed the independence of Puerto Rico, adopted a republican constitution, and established a provisional government. The republic's first official act was to abolish slavery and the *libreta* system. The next day, the rebels attempted to occupy the nearby town of San Sebastián del Pepino, but Spanish troops forced them to retreat and disperse. Governor Julián Pavía quickly directed military operations and imprisoned more than six hundred persons associated with the conspiracy. The Lares insurrection was crushed in less than a month.

The Lares uprising failed to achieve Puerto Rico's independence for several reasons. First, it was hastily organized, ill-equipped, and poorly financed. Second, most of the insurgent leaders were inexperienced in military affairs and could not effectively challenge Spanish troops. Third, the insurrection did not rally wide support from the Puerto Rican population, especially the peasantry. Finally, Spanish colonial authorities ruthlessly persecuted and incarcerated any potential sympathizers with the conspiracy.

Although the rebellion was a military fiasco for the pro-independence movement, it had an enduring impact on subsequent Puerto Rican history. The Lares uprising represented the radicalization of a sector of the Creole elite, which became increasingly distanced from the *peninsulares* (those born in the Iberian Peninsula), especially colonial administrators and merchants. The Creoles' grievances ranged from their exclusion from an authoritarian military government to Spain's monopoly over colonial trade. More broadly, the uprising expressed a growing national consciousness in Puerto Rico, which could draw together various sectors of the Island's population, such as professionals, landowners, peasants, workers, and slaves. Lastly, the Lares revolt became a core symbol for the Island's independence struggle, including the public display of the first national flag of Puerto Rico, modeled after that of the Dominican Republic.

Who was Ramón Emeterio Betances?

Ramón Emeterio Betances (1827–98) was one of the towering political figures in nineteenth-century Puerto Rico. Born to a wealthy landowning and racially mixed family in Cabo Rojo, Betances earned a medical degree from the University of Paris in 1856. He then returned home but had to go back to France the next year, after founding a secret abolitionist society and being banned from the Island for his abolitionist activities. Returning to Puerto Rico in 1859, he opened a surgery practice in Mayagüez, but had to flee again to Santo Domingo in 1862 and to St. Thomas in 1867, where he organized an armed expedition for the aborted insurrection against the Spanish government in Lares in 1868. Again he sought refuge in New York City in 1869, where he joined the Cuban revolutionary movement, and eventually relocated to France, where he died in exile decades later.

Betances is widely regarded as "the father of the homeland" in Puerto Rico. He embraced the philosophy of freemasonry in his steadfast support of liberal reforms and used his international Masonic connections to promote his pro-independence agenda. Today, Betances is still remembered for his 1867 proclamation, "The Ten Commandments of Free Men," advocating the abolition of slavery and civil liberties for all. Betances also proposed an "Antillean confederation," whereby Puerto Rico, Cuba, and the Dominican Republic would establish a regional alliance to preserve their sovereignty and well-being. In addition to numerous political speeches and newspaper articles, Betances wrote several novels, poems, and medical texts in French. For his literary contributions, the French government awarded him the rank of knight of the Legion of Honor in 1887.

How did an incipient sense of national identity emerge on the Island during the nineteenth century?

By the late eighteenth century, most of the Island's inhabitants called themselves *criollos* (Creoles), to distinguish themselves from *peninsulares*, those born in Spain. The term Creole gradually embraced anyone born and raised in the colony, regardless of race and class. Another common expression pitted "those from this side" (*los de la banda de acá*) against "those from the other side" (*los de la banda de allá*). This opposition sharpened throughout the nineteenth century, especially among professionals, intellectuals, and other members of the Creole elite. As in the rest of Spanish America, the gulf between *criollos* and *peninsulares* was based on the exclusion of the natives of the colonies from the highest governmental, military, commercial, and religious posts, since the colonial system accorded special privileges to those born in the metropole. In Puerto Rico, the *peninsulares* held a legal monopoly over colonial trade, the state bureaucracy, and the clergy, while the *criollos* were the principal landholders and professionals.

Cultural expressions such as literature, music, and painting began to reflect a growing sense of Creole identity in Puerto Rico during the nineteenth century. After the introduction of the printing press in 1806, several periodicals such as *La Gaceta de Puerto Rico* and the *Boletín Mercantil* published the first literary texts, especially poems, on the Island. Literary critics usually take the publication of the *Aguinaldo puertorriqueño* (*The Puerto Rican Christmas Gift*, 1843) and the *Album Puertorriqueño* (1844) as the point of departure for an emergent national consciousness. Both volumes contained poems, short stories, and essays authored by Puerto Rican university students in Spain who expressed a strong attachment to their homeland. Among the young authors were José Julián Acosta (1825–91) and Manuel Alonso (1822–89).

Alonso's *El gíbaro* (*The Peasant*, 1849) is widely considered as the founding text of Puerto Rican literature. Alonso exalted the *jíbaros*, their unlettered dialect, and picturesque customs as emblems of Puerto Rican culture, which were enshrined in the Island's literature until the mid-twentieth century. In particular, the work imitated the peasants' speech patterns, including their pronunciation, vocabulary, and syntax. The author also described twenty-one scenes from colonial life, both in poetry and in prose, recreating folk traditions such as *parrandas* (Christmas carols), cockfights, and horseracing.

Alonso's pioneering efforts inaugurated a romantic literary movement on the Island, prolonged by such writers as Alejandro Tapia y Rivera (1826–82), Lola Rodríguez de Tió (1843–1924), and José Gautier Benítez (1849–80). These authors extolled the Island's lush tropical nature, the love of the fatherland, and its cultural values. Many of them were founding members of the Puerto Rican Athenaeum, established in San Juan in 1876 to promote Puerto Rican literature, arts, science, and technology. Other writers, such as Eugenio María de Hostos (1839–1903) and Manuel Zeno Gandía (1855–1930), authored classic works of fiction and nonfiction, which are now part of the literary canon in Puerto Rico. The image of the "Great Puerto Rican Family" became a recurrent theme, focused on the idealization of the *jíbaro*, as a way to bring together people of different class and racial backgrounds.

The plastic arts and music also contributed to portraying Puerto Rican national identity. The mulatto painter José Campeche produced an extraordinary body of work during the second half of the eighteenth century, originating a Creole artistic tradition. The most significant painter of the nineteenth century, Francisco Oller (1833–1917), combined impressionism and realism in his memorable depictions of Puerto Rican landscapes and people. Manuel Gregorio Tavárez (1843–83) has been touted as "the father of the Puerto Rican *danza*," the leading ballroom dance on the Island in the late nineteenth century. Juan Morel Campos (1857–96), the most prolific Puerto Rican composer of his time, authored 283 *danzas*, including the romantic works *Maldito amor* (*Damned Love*, 1884) and *Felices días* (*Happy Days*, 1894). Puerto Rico's national anthem, *La Borinqueña*, is a *danza* composed in 1867, credited to Félix Astol Artés.

Who was Francisco Oller?

Born in Bayamón to a prominent Creole family, Francisco Oller became the leading portrait and landscape artist of his generation in Puerto Rico. After receiving his initial artistic education in San Juan, he studied painting at the San Fernando Royal Academy of Fine Arts in Madrid. He later traveled to Paris to continue his artistic training under Thomas Couture, Gustave Courbet, and other French masters. He also met the leaders of the emerging impressionist movement, such as Claude Monet, Paul Cézanne, and Camille Pissarro. For years Oller moved back and forth between Europe and Puerto Rico, where he established several short-lived art schools, and where he settled permanently in 1884.

Oller's prolific career straddled the realist and impressionist movements, dominant during his lifetime. From his realist mentor Courbet, Oller learned to depict ordinary scenes from the daily life of his homeland, including its people, landscapes, and customs. With his impressionist friends, Oller shared an interest in how light and color shaped perception. His still lifes lovingly recreated the Island's tropical fruits, including coconuts, green plantains, bananas, pineapples, guavas, and soursops. His painting, *The Student* (1874), is the only impressionist work by a Latin American artist at the Musée d'Orsay in Paris. *The School of the Teacher Rafael Cordero* (1892) focuses on a black man who provided free education to the children of San Juan. His masterpiece, *The Wake* (1893), is an ironic rendering of the traditional custom of the *baquiné*, a religious ceremony held after a child's death. Today, several schools, libraries, and museums in Puerto Rico and the United States are named after Oller, including a museum in Bayamón that features several portraits by the city's most famous native son.

How did folk music contribute to the expression of Puerto Rican cultural identity?

Puerto Ricans developed several musical practices during the Spanish colonial period. Among these genres, the *seis* is one of Puerto Rico's best-known—and most Spanish—song types. The *seis* formed the backbone of Puerto Rican country music, and one of its variants, the *seis chorreao*, was the preferred dance among the peasants. The *seis* is usually sung in *décimas*—stanzas with ten octosyllabic lines and an alternating rhyme structure. *Décimas* began to be cultivated in sixteenth-century Spain and became one of the favorite poetic forms in Puerto Rico. The instruments used to accompany the *seis* are the guitar, the *cuatro* (a smaller Creole version of the Spanish guitar), and the *güiro* (the indigenous percussion instrument). The *seis* is in simple duple meter based on a single musical motive. Many of its themes can be traced back to the medieval

and Renaissance *romances* common during the Spanish colonization of Puerto Rico. Some *seises* preserve intact the melodies
of Golden Age songs from Andalusia and Extremadura.

The *seis* and the many variations it engendered (*seis de
bomba, seis pañuelo, seis bayamonés*) are distinctive of a particular geographic and socioeconomic sphere in Puerto Rico.
Ecologically, the *seis* belongs to the mountainous central areas
of the Island where coffee and tobacco became the dominant
cash crops. Sociologically, it is the musical expression of a large
class of subsistence farmers and sharecroppers. Culturally, it
remains attached to its Spanish colonial models, fundamen-
tally of Andalusian, Extremaduran, and Canary Island origin.
Like other rural genres, the music of the *jíbaros* is basically conservative in maintaining traditional melodies and rhythms,
and innovative mainly in text composition.

The *bomba* dance, on the other hand, has unmistakable
African roots, specifically in the Guinea Coast of West Africa,
and is closely related to Ghanan, Haitian, and French Antillean
genres such as the Martinican *vidié*. The *bomba* probably originated with the immigration of French planters and slaves from
St. Domingue (Haiti), Louisiana, and other Caribbean territories after 1815. The French/Haitian origin of some *bomba*
dances is clear in the names of six subtypes known as *bamulé,
calinde, cuayá, grasimá, leró*, and *sicá*. Some *bomba* songs may
have Haitian Creole lyrics, and the *bombas* danced around the
Loíza Aldea area resemble French Antillean types.

The *bomba* synthesizes several African musical currents as
they converged in the plantation environment. It is characterized by melodic repetition and complex rhythm; by an antiphonal structure and the use of the pentatonic scale; by duple
meter and the predominance of percussion. The *bomba* uses the
onomatopoeic and rhythmic values of the human voice, and its
lyrics are designed to follow and emphasize the rhythm. That
is, words are employed primarily for their phonetic rather
than their semantic value. The chorus sings in unison, and
harmony is altogether absent. It is often polyrhythmic and is

accompanied by two drums called *bombas*, two sticks (*claves*), and a *maraca*.

Bombas were sung and danced principally around sugar mill areas, on Saturday evenings and other holidays such as the closing of the harvest season (the *zafra*). Hence they were closely tied to the plantation's life cycle and followed the ebbs and flows of the sugar industry. The *bomba* was not as widely accepted as the *seis* or the *plena*, but was confined mostly to the coastal lowlands. Today it is still danced in towns like Loíza, Fajardo, Guayama, and Salinas, where the percentage of people of African ancestry is larger than elsewhere.

At the other end of the spectrum, the Puerto Rican *danza* originated within the nineteenth-century Creole aristocracy. This elite salon dance is closely linked to the Cuban *habanera* and the French *contradanse* that were widely popular at the time. The lower classes have appropriated some classical *danzas*, such as those composed by Morel Campos. But the commonly held definition of acceptable music in Puerto Rican society today lies somewhere in between the two poles of the *danza* and the *bomba*. It would take a mulatto synthesis such as the *plena*—or, later on, salsa—to reach a wide audience among working-class Puerto Ricans.

The *plena*, like the *bomba*, has many African elements. It consists of an alternating scheme between the soloist and the chorus, in the antiphonal style characteristic of most West African songs. Both rhythmic and textual improvisation are important aspects of its performance. It often utilizes diatonic melodies and even eight-beat phrases in a syncopated duple meter. The instruments used to accompany it may be those of any typical dance orchestra, but they must at least include two *panderetas* or tambourines.

The *plena* also displays non-African elements. The lyrics usually follow Spanish rhetorical forms such as the *cuarteta* or the *sextilla*. Like the Spanish *romance*, the *plena* chronicles memorable or unusual events taken from the contemporary scene. A kind of musical newspaper, the *plena* dwells on the topics that most impress coastal residents, ranging from every-day incidents to international happenings. History and legend mingle in *plena* lyrics, whose essential character can be described as simple, direct, and epigrammatic, and their general tone as playful and ironic.

How was slavery abolished in Puerto Rico?

In 1873, Spain finally ended slavery in Puerto Rico, one of the last remaining slave territories in the New World (only Cuba and Brazil abolished slavery later). The emancipation of slaves was one of the main political projects of Puerto Rican liberals during the nineteenth century. During the first half of the century, a growing number of prominent Puerto Ricans advocated abolition, in opposition to the dominant current in the Spanish metropolitan government. Abolitionism found fertile ground among the children of Puerto Rican slaveholding families who pursued higher education in Spain, where they were exposed to liberal reformist ideas. After 1850, the abolitionist movement gained strength, led by such professionals as Betances and Segundo Ruiz Belvis (1829–67). Several secret societies, particularly Masonic lodges, promoted the emancipation of slaves, especially in cities along the western coast of Puerto Rico, such as Mayagüez and Cabo Rojo. In 1865, José Julián Acosta, Román Baldorioty de Castro (1822–89), and Julio Vizcarrondo (1829–89) founded the Spanish Abolitionist Society in Madrid, to promote the liberation of slaves in the Spanish Antilles.

From 1845 to its abolition in 1873, slavery gradually lost ground to "free" labor in Puerto Rico, although much of it was coerced during the *libreta* regime. Compared with other Caribbean societies such as Jamaica or Cuba, Puerto Rico had a much larger "free colored" population. By 1860, that population, classified as *parda* (racially mixed), represented 41.3 percent of the Island's inhabitants. Thus, wage workers of various origins—predominantly those born in Puerto Rico—replaced slaves imported from Africa for nearly four centuries. The relatively small number of slaves (29,335 in 1873) on the Island facilitated their emancipation.

How did the 1897 Autonomous Charter define Puerto Rico's political status under Spain?

For decades, Puerto Rican autonomists had struggled for increased participation in the Island's colonial administration. Strained by Cuba's revolutionary war, beginning in 1895, and anticipating a possible US intervention, a liberal Spanish government finally responded to the autonomists' demands. On November 25, 1897, the Queen Regent María Cristina signed the Autonomous Charter granting Puerto Rico more self-government than ever before or after. The charter allowed Puerto Rico (as well as Cuba) to elect its own parliament, increase its representation in the Spanish parliament, enter into international trade treaties, impose its own import and export tariffs, enjoy the same citizenship rights as peninsular Spain, and receive full legal protection under the Spanish Constitution. On February 9, 1898, a new government of Puerto Rico was inaugurated under the Autonomous Charter. Six months later, the war between the United States and Spain shattered Puerto Rico's hopes for self-determination. On December 1, 1898, Spain ceded Puerto Rico (as well as the Philippines and Guam) as war booty to the United States.

Why was the United States interested in Puerto Rico?

Since the end of the eighteenth century, US policymakers had expressed an interest in purchasing or annexing Puerto Rico and other Caribbean territories, especially Cuba, Santo Domingo, and Haiti. In 1783, John Adams, the future second president of the United States, asserted that both Cuba and Puerto Rico were an integral part of US trade in the Caribbean.

His son, John Quincy Adams, then Secretary of State and later the sixth US president, reiterated in 1823 that the two islands were "natural appendages to the North American continent." The United States developed strong commercial ties to Puerto Rico during the first half of the nineteenth century, especially as the main export market for the Island's growing sugar industry.

By the end of the nineteenth century, Puerto Rico was considered key to the geopolitical and economic ambitions of the United States. To become a world naval power, the United States had to secure coaling stations and naval bases in the Caribbean and the Pacific. Since the 1890s, US foreign policy in the Caribbean Basin centered on the need to construct and protect a transisthmian canal across Central America. After the end of the Spanish-Cuban-American War, US naval strategists such as Alfred T. Mahan underscored the military significance of Puerto Rico as "the Malta of the Caribbean," the guardian of the Mona Passage, one of the main routes between the Caribbean Sea and the Atlantic Ocean. With the proposed construction of the Panama Canal, the Island acquired greater strategic importance. Retaining US control over Puerto Rico ensured a permanent naval base in the Caribbean.

US corporate interests coincided with the geopolitical imperative of consolidating US naval power in the Caribbean. At least since 1830, the United States had replaced Spain as Puerto Rico's main trade partner and remained so for most of the nineteenth century. The Island was deemed a lucrative overseas market for US manufactured goods, as well as a provider of raw materials and tropical commodities, especially sugar cane. Sugar was one of the few key commodities in which the United States was not self-sufficient. Thus, the US occupation of Puerto Rico in 1898 was part of a broader policy to expand the US geopolitical and economic presence in the "American Mediterranean." Once again, the Island's strategic location would help determine its fate.

2

PUERTO RICO UNDER US RULE, 1898–1952

How did the US government acquire the Island?

On July 25, 1898, US troops invaded Puerto Rico as part of the war against Spain. The Island was a secondary military asset to US objectives (Cuba was the primary target at the time). After a brief military campaign, the United States and Spain signed the Treaty of Paris on December 10, 1898, where Spain ceded Puerto Rico (as well as the Philippines and Guam) to the United States. Cuba was temporarily transferred under US tutelage but became independent in 1902. The "splendid little war" (in Theodore Roosevelt's famous quip) extended the territorial boundaries of the United States well beyond the North American continent. The Treaty of Paris stipulated that the US Congress would determine the civil rights and political status of Puerto Rico and the other newly acquired territories. Puerto Rico became an overseas possession of the United States without any representation of the Island's inhabitants in the peace negotiation.

The acquisition of the new territories sparked intense legal and political debates in the United States. To begin, the federal government followed a different approach to its new acquisitions, insofar as it did not promise them statehood. Unlike in earlier territories, including Hawaii, the US Constitution was not applied equally to Puerto Rico and other overseas possessions. The US Supreme Court eventually devised a new legal category—that of "unincorporated territory"—to justify the "plenary" or absolute power of the US Congress over the insular possessions. Finally, the Philippines became independent in 1946, while the United States retained Puerto Rico and Guam (as well as the US Virgin Islands, acquired in 1917) as unincorporated territories, which the US Supreme Court declared to "belong to but not be a part of" the United States. This equivocal legal status continues to haunt the Island today.

How did Puerto Ricans initially receive the US occupying forces?

According to historical accounts, US troops did not encounter much resistance throughout the Island; most Puerto Ricans greeted them with joy and enthusiasm. During the first months of the US occupation, the prevailing mood on the Island was one of optimism and expectation. Most of the Island's political leaders welcomed the representatives of the United States as personifying democratic and modern values. Local merchants, landowners, and professionals were eager to reap the economic and political benefits of Puerto Rico's annexation to the United States. Workers, too, saw an opportunity in integrating into US trade unions and expanding their labor rights. Puerto Ricans of various social classes regarded the US occupation as a positive break with Spanish colonialism, which they considered authoritarian and retrograde. Unfortunately, public perceptions of the United States as progressive liberators quickly vanished, with the prolongation of a military government between 1898 and 1900 and the approval of the Foraker Act in 1900.

How did the United States govern Puerto Rico between 1898 and 1952?

After the Island's occupation, the US Department of War quickly dismantled the short-lived autonomous government established in Puerto Rico under Spanish rule in 1897. The United States governed the Island under a military administration between July 26, 1898 and May 1, 1900. Several military decrees and two organic laws, the Foraker Act of 1900 and the Jones Act of 1917, regulated relations between Puerto Rico and the United States. Until 1948–52, Puerto Ricans had little say in their own government; the governor, most members of the executive cabinet, and the justices of the Supreme Court of Puerto Rico were Americans appointed by the president of the United States. Only one US governor, Theodore Roosevelt, Jr. (1887–1944), made an effort to learn Spanish to communicate with the Puerto Rican people. He was also critical of colonial policies on the Island. Although the US government eschewed the term "colonialism" to refer to Puerto Rico and its overseas possessions, it ruled them much like other colonies throughout the world, without significant participation by the governed subjects.

What was the Foraker Act of 1900?

The Foraker Act, also known as the First Organic Act, established the legal framework for a civil government in Puerto Rico under US tutelage. It marked a sharp rupture with the existing US policy of incorporation of newly acquired territories as the legal basis for eventual statehood. The act made it clear that Puerto Rico was an overseas possession subject to the plenary power of the US Congress, but did not commit Congress to extend either independence or statehood to the Island.

The Foraker Act established a highly centralized administrative structure for the government of Puerto Rico, headed by a governor, cabinet, Supreme Court, and other high-ranking members appointed by the US president. Thus, the law concentrated most legislative, executive, and judicial power in the hands of appointed, not elected, officials. Indeed, the president named all of the eleven members of the powerful Executive Council, including six members from the United States and five from Puerto Rico. Relegated to the Executive Council was an insular Chamber of Delegates with thirty-five members elected by Puerto Ricans.

This administrative arrangement allowed for little input by Puerto Ricans into their own government. The Foraker Act actually provided a smaller measure of self-determination than the Autonomous Charter granted by Spain in 1897, before the US occupation of the Island. The US law was based on the presumption that Puerto Ricans were unfit to govern themselves. As a result, white males from the United States headed all of the key local government agencies, including Justice, Labor, Education, and Agriculture, between 1900 and 1917. While the US president named a nonvoting resident commissioner from Puerto Rico to Congress, the latter reserved the right to veto any law passed on the Island. Even though the Foraker Act established free trade between the United States and Puerto Rico, it required that all merchandise be carried by the US Merchant Marine, a legal requirement still in place today. Not surprisingly, many of Puerto Rico's political leaders were disillusioned with the lack of autonomy over their own affairs.

How did the US Supreme Court define Puerto Rico's legal status?

In a series of judicial decisions known as the "Insular Cases" (1901–22), the US Supreme Court addressed the legal status of the newly acquired US territories and their inhabitants. In *Downes v. Bidwell* (1901), the court defined Puerto Rico paradoxically as "foreign to the United States in a domestic sense because the island has not been incorporated into the United States, but was merely appurtenant thereto as a possession." In particular, the court determined that "the Island of Porto Rico [sic] is not a part of the United States within that provision of the Constitution which declares that 'all duties, imposts, and excises shall be uniform throughout the United States.'"

In expressing the court's majority decision, Justice Henry Billings Brown insisted that Puerto Rico was "a territory appurtenant and belonging to ... but not a part of the United States." Based on the spurious distinction between incorporated and unincorporated territories, the court determined that "the constitution does not follow the flag." That is, not all rights, duties, laws, and regulations promulgated by the federal government extended to its overseas possessions. In effect, Puerto Ricans acquired a second-class status, similar to that of African Americans, American Indians, and women before the approval of universal suffrage. The Island's inhabitants were subject to US sovereignty without a clear or permanent relation to the rest of the United States, a confusing legal situation that continues today.

What was the Jones Act of 1917?

The Jones Act, also known as Jones-Shaffron Act or Second Organic Act, granted US citizenship to all Puerto Ricans. The law maintained intact the US colonial regime in Puerto Rico, although it expanded Puerto Rican involvement in the legislative sphere. It replaced the Executive Council with an elected bicameral legislature, composed of a Senate, with nineteen members, and a House of Representatives, with thirty-nine members. The Jones Act granted Puerto Ricans a Bill of Rights, including the right to a speedy and public trial (but not trial by jury); freedom of speech, the press, and religion; and an eight-hour work day. The new law also authorized the election of the Island's resident commissioner, who was previously appointed by the US president.

However, the Jones Act failed to meet the expectations of most Puerto Rican leaders for greater self-government and clarification of the Island's political status. Under the new legislation, Puerto Rico remained an unincorporated territory of the United States and under its shipping laws. The US Congress could annul or amend bills passed by the insular legislature. Most appointed officials on the Island were still US citizens who did not speak Spanish and were unfamiliar with Puerto Rican culture. Some Puerto Ricans could now direct government agencies, but the US president still named most of them. Until the 1940s, nonresident Americans continued to occupy key positions as governors, auditors, and heads of the Departments of Justice and Education.

The Jones Act conferred US citizenship, but not equal political representation, upon Puerto Rico's inhabitants. Furthermore, it did not recognize all their constitutional rights and duties, such as having voting delegates in Congress or paying federal income tax. Moreover, residents of Puerto Rico had no right to a trial by jury, unlike those living in the United States, according to the Sixth Amendment of the US Constitution. Many of the basic elements of the Jones Act remain in effect today, as coded by the Puerto Rico Federal Relations Act of 1950.

What was the impact of extending US citizenship to Puerto Ricans?

The granting of US citizenship to the Island in 1917 has been one of the most influential decisions regarding the political future of Puerto Ricans. As Congressman William Jones (the sponsor of the Jones Act) argued in 1914, his proposed bill was primarily designed to ensure that the Island "remain a permanent possession of the United States." The implementation of the Jones Act also had military implications. The US Congress approved the bill in March 1917 and a month later declared war on the German empire. During World War I, Puerto Ricans were required to register for military service, and 17,855 were drafted at the time, many of them to guard the Panama Canal Zone. Hundreds of thousands of Puerto Ricans have served in the US armed forces in all major US wars since then. Military service continues to be a major source of employment and upward social mobility for Puerto Rican youth today.

Originally an external imposition by Congress, US citizenship has become one of the ideological pillars of permanent association between Puerto Rico and the United States. Moreover, the discourse of rights is a powerful ideological justification for the Island's complete annexation into the American union. Today, most Puerto Ricans recognize the material and symbolic value of US citizenship, including access to federally funded programs; unrestricted movement between the Island and the mainland; and protection of some of the civil, social, and political rights guaranteed by the Constitution of the United States.

What are the limitations of US citizenship for residents of Puerto Rico?

Puerto Ricans living on the Island cannot exercise the full range of constitutional rights as US citizens living in the mainland, such as voting for federal officials. However, they can do so if they relocate to one of the fifty states. Because all Puerto Ricans are US citizens by birth, they have the right of abode in the continental United States, Hawaii, and other overseas possessions of the United States. Since the early twentieth century, place of residence has determined the extent to which Puerto Ricans enjoy their rights as US citizens. This territorially grounded distinction in citizenship rights remains a defining characteristic of US colonialism on the Island.

Why did the US colonial government encourage migration?

Soon after the US occupation of Puerto Rico, the colonial regime began to promote the relocation of workers from the Island. This public policy was based on the widespread perception that Puerto Rico was a small, poor, and overcrowded country with few natural resources. Early efforts focused on transporting Puerto Ricans to other Caribbean and Pacific territories under US hegemony, such as Hawaii, Cuba, the

Dominican Republic, and the US Virgin Islands, particularly St. Croix.

The first civilian US governor, Charles Allen, wrote in 1902, "Porto Rico [sic] has plenty of laborers and poor people generally. What the island needs is men with capital, energy, and enterprise." In 1912, Governor Arthur Yager held that "the only really effective remedy [to the problem of overpopulation] is the transfer of large numbers of Porto Ricans to another region." In 1917 General Frank McIntyre, chief of the Bureau of Insular Affairs, favored "the colonizing of several hundred thousand of the Porto Rican people in Santo Domingo." A 1919 report for the US Department of Labor pondered migration to the Dominican Republic and Cuba, but concluded that "it falls short of its purpose when submitted to careful analysis." Instead, the report recommended establishing an office of the US Employment Service in Puerto Rico to facilitate the relocation of Puerto Ricans to the United States. Three decades later, the Committee on Insular Affairs of the US House of Representatives endorsed "a wise and prudent program of emigration" to alleviate the Island's "lack of natural resources" and "congestion of population."

How did the sugar plantation model expand and later decline on the Island?

The US occupation of Puerto Rico in 1898 and its subsequent colonial administration transformed the whole agrarian structure to suit the demands of huge sugar corporations, or *centrales*. These enterprises tended to concentrate landownership into a few large estates (*latifundios*), especially in the coastal lowlands, thus reversing an earlier trend toward the dispersion of property. In less than ten years, the seigneurial *hacienda* economy was converted into a modern plantation system. By 1930 the agrarian transformation was complete: Puerto Rico was a typical Caribbean sugar island, characterized by the extreme concentration of land and capital, the predominance of capitalist relations of production, the lack of internal economic diversification, the production of a primary commodity for a single external market, and the import of most basic goods from the metropole.

The sugar industry was the principal beneficiary of the new economic scenario inaugurated by the US occupation of Puerto Rico. Direct US political control and free trade between the United States and Puerto Rico attracted growing US investment in sugar agriculture, which enjoyed duty-free entry into the United States. Between 1901 and 1932, the Island's share of the US sugar market soared from 2.1 percent to 14.6 percent. The value of sugar exports rose from $4.7 million to almost $53.7 million between 1901 and 1930. Four large US corporations (South Porto Rico, United Porto Rico/Eastern Sugar, Fajardo, and Central Aguirre) produced more than 51 percent of the Island's sugar harvest in 1927–28. These companies owned or leased 23.7 percent of all cane land in Puerto Rico in 1930.

The main economic casualty of the US occupation of Puerto Rico was the coffee industry, which had become the Island's chief export in the late nineteenth century. In 1896, coffee made up 76.9 percent of Puerto Rico's total exports; by 1930 it represented less than one percent. Between 1901 and 1935, the value of Puerto Rico's coffee exports plunged from $1.7 million to less than $208,000. The Island's inclusion within the US tariff system made exporting Puerto Rican coffee too expensive to its traditional European and Cuban markets, as well as any potential new markets in the United States. Moreover, world prices for coffee fell with the expansion of production in Brazil, as well as other Central and South American countries. After a brief recovery during World War I, coffee prices continued to decline. Furthermore, US consumers preferred the weaker taste of South American coffee, compared to the stronger, richer coffee produced in Puerto Rico. Since the 1930s, the Island became a net importer of coffee to meet a growing local demand.

Unable to eke out an existence from the soil, landless farmers and *hacienda* workers began to move from the coffee highlands to the sugar plantations and the towns and cities on the coast, which were fast becoming the dynamic centers of the economy. Many left for the United States, other parts of the Caribbean, and Hawaii. During the nineteenth century people migrated to the central highlands in search of better economic opportunities; in the twentieth century many took the road back to the coast for the same reason.

The Great Depression of 1929–33 shook the foundations of the Island's plantation system. Puerto Rico's sugar industry never recovered from that international crisis of the capitalist market, and has undergone progressive deterioration ever since. In the 1930s, the federal government extended the New Deal to the Island through the Puerto Rican Emergency Relief Administration (PRERA) and the Puerto Rican Reconstruction Administration (PRRA). These two agencies provided temporary relief and grants and loans for public works in a distressed economy. Nonetheless, commercial agriculture continued its long-term decay on the Island.

During the 1930s and 1940s, more rural dwellers migrated to the cities, especially to San Juan's growing squatter settlements (*arrabales*). Former peons, sharecroppers, small farmers, and rural wage laborers fled the countryside, particularly from the coffee-growing regions of the interior to the coastal cities, especially to the peripheries of major urban centers. The crisis of the agricultural sector nourished Puerto Rico's urban working classes.

What was the significance of Puerto Rico's tobacco industry during the first third of the twentieth century?

Puerto Rico's inclusion within the US tariff system and increasing US investment stimulated tobacco growing and cigar manufacturing on the Island after 1898. The number of *cuerdas* (one *cuerda* is equivalent to 0.971 acres) devoted to the cultivation of tobacco rose from 5,963 in 1899 to 81,900 in 1927. The number of tobacco farms also increased from 26,736 in 1910 to 30,104 in 1940. Between 1907 and 1917, tobacco was the third-largest cash crop in Puerto Rico, after sugar and coffee. In 1918, tobacco displaced coffee as the Island's second-leading export and remained so between 1921 and 1940.

Cultivated by the Taínos since pre-Columbian times, tobacco was well suited to Puerto Rico's mountainous terrain. It was predominantly grown in the eastern and western highlands, from San Lorenzo to Utuado, particularly in Caguas, Cayey, Barranquitas, and Comerío. It became known as "the poor man's crop" because it required little capital and machinery and had low production costs. Most tobacco growers were small independent farmers who owned less than fifteen *cuerdas* of land. They usually planted tobacco in combination with subsistence crops such as corn, rice, green beans, plantains, and sweet potatoes. They also raised goats, chicken, and pigs. During the early twentieth century, the population of the tobacco-growing districts grew faster than elsewhere, as many people moved to those areas in search of economic opportunities.

The US invasion of the Island also accelerated the concentration of cigar manufacturing in large factories, especially those with more than one hundred workers. Most of these factories were located in budding urban centers, such as Puerta de Tierra in San Juan and Caguas in the center of the Island. They attracted a growing number of women workers, who usually assumed the worst-paid occupations within the industry, such as stemmers (*despalilladoras*); men dominated the craft of cigar-making. By 1910, cigar manufacturing was the largest employer of Puerto Rican women (11,118). Between 1899 and 1930, the number of women workers in cigar factories increased from 60 to 9,290. During this period, cigar workers, both male and female, became engaged in trade unions and socialist and anarchist organizations.

Most of Puerto Rico's tobacco was destined for the US market, especially as filler (*tripa*) for cigars manufactured in mainland factories. Unfortunately, US demand for the Island's tobacco plummeted in the 1930s, as smokers shifted their preference from cigars to cigarettes made from tobacco from other places. In particular, the production of shade-grown wrapper tobacco became unprofitable after 1927. Moreover, cigarettes imported from the United States flooded the Puerto Rican market during the 1930s. Accordingly, the value of tobacco exports fell from 17.5 percent of the Island's total exports in 1931 to 6.6 percent in 1940. Employment in cigar manufacturing declined from 7,543 in 1909–10 to only 539 in 1939–40. Puerto Rico's tobacco industry never recovered from this precipitous decline.

How did the US colonial government attempt to Americanize Puerto Ricans?

Between 1898 and 1948, the US colonial regime sought to make Puerto Ricans identify with US interests and acquire American culture, particularly through the teaching of English and the abandonment of Puerto Rican history and customs. US colonial policy implied that the dominant language, culture, and religion of the United States were morally superior to those of Spain. The Island would be Americanized through the influx of US capital, businesses, technology, laws, ideas, and customs. US colonial administrators even anglicized the Island's Spanish name to "Porto Rico." Most official and journalistic reports about the Island retained the US spelling until 1932, when the US Congress passed a resolution adopting the official name of Puerto Rico.

The Island's Department of Education was the main vehicle for suppressing Spanish and implanting English. Between 1903 and 1916, teachers were expected to use English as the sole language of instruction in all subject matters, beginning in the third grade. Later, English and Spanish were combined to differing degrees in public schools. Given the scarcity of local teachers who could teach in English, hundreds of teachers were recruited in the United States. At the same time,

Puerto Rican teachers were sent to the mainland during the summers to learn English. To this day, teachers are often called "Mr." and "Mrs." (in English) on the Island.

In addition, schools were named after US heroes such as George Washington, Thomas Jefferson, Abraham Lincoln, and Benjamin Franklin. School buildings often followed California's Mission and Florida's Spanish Revival architectural styles. School curricula and textbooks were imported from the United States without major adaptations. Puerto Rican schoolchildren were taught to salute the US flag, listen to the US anthem, swear the oath of allegiance to the United States, and sing US patriotic songs. US holidays such as the Fourth of July were officially commemorated in Puerto Rico. The school calendar did not observe the longstanding Christmas celebration of the Epiphany (Three Kings' Day on January 6th). No holidays were held in honor of Puerto Rican public figures until well into the twentieth century.

How did Puerto Ricans resist US colonialism?

Defending the Spanish language became one of the rallying cries against Americanization. This resistance brought together broad sectors of the population, including teachers, students, and intellectuals. Since its inception in 1911, the Puerto Rican Teachers' Association protested the use of English as the language of instruction and advocated for the adoption of the Spanish vernacular as the Island's official language. In the end, the Americanization campaign was largely a failure, insofar as most Puerto Ricans did not become fluent English speakers. Instead, linguistic nationalism—Hispanic in nature—gradually became the dominant ideology on the Island. For decades, leaders of the main political parties in Puerto Rico have agreed that preserving the Spanish language is non-negotiable under any political formula.

Another gesture of defiance involved the assertion of the icons of Puerto Rican nationhood. Between 1898 and 1952, the public use of the Puerto Rican flag was banned on the Island. Law 53 of 1948—better known as the "Gag Law"—made it a felony to own and display a Puerto Rican flag, even in one's home. The original lyrics of the anthem *La Borinqueña*, written in 1868 by Lola Rodríguez Tió, were considered too subversive and were replaced by less confrontational ones by Manuel Fernández Juncos (1846–1928) in 1903. The national flag and anthem became official symbols of Puerto Rico with the Commonwealth's establishment in 1952.

Since 1898, national identity in Puerto Rico has developed mostly under—and sometimes in outright opposition to—US hegemony. A minority of the Island's population assumed a violent resistance to US colonialism. Among the most militant groups were members of the Nationalist Party, from the 1930s to the 1950s. Although small in number and electoral significance, the Nationalist Party reflected widespread social discontent, labor unrest, and anti-colonialist resentment. US and Puerto Rican authorities responded with increasing repression and persecution of nationalists. Between 1948 and 1957, the Gag Law prohibited the expression of ideas and acts against the US government and in favor of Puerto Rico's independence.

Who was Luisa Capetillo?

Luisa Capetillo (1879–1922) was a pioneering feminist, anarchist, labor leader, journalist, and writer. Born in Arecibo, Puerto Rico, to a Spanish immigrant father and a French immigrant mother, she began working at a young age in the garment industry. She also became a *lectora* (reader) in the cigar factories of her hometown, a prestigious occupation that involved reading aloud newspaper articles and classic works of literature, philosophy, and politics while workers rolled their cigars.

Between 1907 and 1917, Capetillo authored four books, including the earliest feminist treatise published in Puerto Rico,

Mi opinión sobre las libertades, derechos y deberes de la mujer (*My Opinion about the Freedoms, Rights, and Duties of Women*, 1911/ 1913). In 1912 she moved to New York City, where she was a labor organizer; the next year she relocated to Tampa, Florida, where she resumed her work as a *lectora* in cigar factories. She later lived in Havana, Cuba, where she was arrested in 1915 for being the first woman to wear trousers in public. For several years she moved back and forth between San Juan and New York City, until she resettled in Puerto Rico in 1920. She died of tuberculosis two years later.

By the 1920s, Capetillo became well known within literary, feminist, and labor circles on the Island and abroad. Today, she is mostly remembered for her radical beliefs in free love, sexual liberation, and women's education. Throughout her life and work she questioned conventional norms of gender relations, particularly middle-class notions of the family that, in her view, oppressed women. She also denounced the Catholic Church because of its endorsement of repressive regimes, embraced the Spiritist philosophy of Alan Kardec, and advocated for the rights of workers and women, especially in Puerto Rico, the Caribbean, and the United States.

How did the socioeconomic position of Puerto Rican women change during the first half of the twentieth century?

The US occupation of the Island accelerated women's incorporation into the paid labor force. In 1899, 86 percent of all employed women were concentrated in three service occupations: domestics, laundresses, and dressmakers and seamstresses. Paid domestic work remained the main source of female employment during the first four decades of the twentieth century. Domestic service still represented 28.2 percent of all employed women in 1940. The cigar industry also employed a growing number of women between 1910 and 1935. With the expansion of the educational system, teaching offered new professional opportunities for women, together with clerical work, nursing, and social work. Between 1899 and 1930, female labor force participation rose from 9.9 percent to 26.1 percent. During the 1930s the home needlework industry, which drew primarily on seamstresses and embroiderers, became the second leading sector of the Island's economy, both in terms of the volume of exports and the number of jobs. Overall, Puerto Rican women clustered in low-paying and low-status occupations that extended their traditional duties and skills as housemakers, wives, and mothers.

The struggle for women's right to vote was a major social movement during the first three decades of the twentieth century. In 1917, the Puerto Rican Feminine League (*Liga Femínea Puertorriqueña*) became the first organization to promote women's right to vote on the Island, followed by the Puerto Rican Association of Suffragist Women (*Asociación Puertorriqueña de Mujeres Sufragistas*) in 1925. Many suffragist leaders (such as Ana Roque de Duprey [1853–1923] and Isabel Andreu de Aguilar [1887–1948]) were teachers. The suffragist movement was primarily oriented toward liberal reforms that would increase middle-class women's access to higher education and public life. Few working-class women were suffragist leaders and were better represented in the labor movement. Unfortunately, the Nineteenth Amendment to the US Constitution, granting all women the right to vote, ratified in 1920, was not extended to Puerto Rico. In 1929, the insular legislature approved a law granting the right to vote to women who could read and write. Universal suffrage was finally attained on the Island in 1935.

How did the Generation of 1930 contribute to Puerto Rico's national culture?

The Generation of 1930, a notable group of writers, scholars, and professors that included Antonio S. Pedreira (1899–1939),

Tomás Blanco (1896–1975), Vicente Géigel Polanco (1903–79), and Margot Arce de Vázquez (1904–90), established the Island's modern literary canon. This tightly knit clique of professionals constituted an intellectual field, dominated by cultural nationalism, primarily based on Puerto Rico's Hispanic heritage.

A foundational text in the development of the Island's nationalist discourse is Antonio Pedreira's *Insularismo* or *Insularism*, first published in 1934 and reprinted several times later. A distinguished professor of Spanish literature at the University of Puerto Rico, Pedreira was an ideological heir to the moderate autonomist tradition of the nineteenth-century Creole elite, rather than radical separatism from Spain. In this book, he posed the key questions, "What are we? or how are we Puerto Ricans, globally considered?" He answered in three main ways: (1) culturally, Puerto Rico is a Hispanic colony; (2) racially, it is an extremely mixed and confused population; and (3) geographically, it is an island marginalized from world history. According to Pedreira, territorial isolation primarily molded the Puerto Rican character; hence the title emphasizing insularity. The Island's geographic situation conditioned Puerto Ricans to feel small, dependent, and passive. In the end, an intense inferiority complex dominated the islanders' collective personality and forced them to rely on more powerful, continental countries like Spain and the United States. Pedreira's philosophical pessimism permeated his entire argument, from the so-called degeneration of the races in a tropical environment to the practical difficulties of leading the Puerto Rican people to an independent state.

Despite its shortcomings, *Insularismo* remains one of the wellsprings of contemporary thinking and writing on the Island's culture. As such, it is part of the dominant narrative of the Puerto Rican nation and required reading on public school curricula. The current intellectual discussion on national identity in Puerto Rico is still framed largely in Pedreira's terms. Now as then, scholars, writers, and artists often feel threatened by the Americanization of Puerto Rican culture. In response to that perceived threat, local intellectuals have tended to reassert the Hispanic roots of Puerto Rican culture and to cultivate Creole topics such as the *jíbaro*, the landscape, and folklore. A "romantic return to the mountains"—as a nationalist leader, Juan Antonio Corretjer (1908–85), titled his 1929 book of poems—characterized much of the Island's literary activity during the first half of the twentieth century, when the dominant emblems of national identity were first defined. As the home of the *jíbaro*, the highlands have long been hailed as the core of Puerto Ricanness. Similarly, until the 1950s the Island's plastic arts were primarily concerned with the creation of a national iconography based on local types, customs, and landscapes. As writers and artists elaborated the dominant representations of Puerto Ricanness, they tended to gloss over the Island's internal diversity. For instance, the *jíbaro* was typically depicted as a white, male, and rural character, at the exclusion of blacks, women, and urban dwellers.

Who was Julia de Burgos?

Julia de Burgos (1914–53) was one of the leading Puerto Rican and Latin American poets of the twentieth century, as well as a journalist, editor, and teacher. Born to a poor family in a rural district of Carolina, Puerto Rico, she earned a teaching certificate at the University of Puerto Rico in 1933 and worked briefly as an elementary schoolteacher. An advocate of independence, she joined the Nationalist Party in 1936 and was elected secretary general of the women's branch of the party. Burgos moved to New York City in 1940 and then to Cuba. She returned to New York in 1942, where she served as arts and culture editor of the journal *Pueblos Hispanos* (*Hispanic Peoples*) between 1943 and 1945. After falling unconscious in the streets of Spanish Harlem, she died of pneumonia in a New York hospital in 1953.

Burgos began to publish her work in Puerto Rican journals and newspapers during the 1930s. Altogether she authored more than two hundred poems, collected in four books (the last one published posthumously in 1954), including *Poema en veinte surcos* (*Poem in Twenty Furrows*, 1938) and *Canción de la verdad sencilla* (*Song of the Simple Truth*, 1939), which established her literary reputation. Many of her texts challenged conventional representations of women, blacks, and peasants in Puerto Rican society. In particular, she denounced patriarchal oppression, social injustice, racism, and colonialism. Whereas some of her poems were politically engaged, others elaborated intimate, erotic, and amorous themes. Except for her last two poems, "Farewell in Welfare Island" and "The Sun in Welfare Island" (1953), Burgos wrote in Spanish. She shared a profound admiration for Hispanic culture with other contemporary intellectuals in Puerto Rico.

Literary critics have interpreted Burgos's work as part of a transitional generation between the Generation of 1930 and the Nuyorican movement during the 1970s. Contemporary US Puerto Rican and Latina writers, such as Sandra María Esteves (b. 1948) and María Teresa "Mariposa" Fernández (b. 1971), consider Burgos a literary precursor. After her untimely death, Burgos became a symbol of resistance to colonialism, sexism, and racism. Her life and work continue to invoke strong feelings of attachment among Puerto Ricans and other Latinos. Many schools, parks, and cultural centers on the Island and in the US mainland are named in her honor.

Who was Luis Muñoz Marín?

Luis Muñoz Marín (1898–1980) was Puerto Rico's dominant political leader during the twentieth century. He was born in San Juan to a prominent autonomist family; his father, Luis Muñoz Rivera (1859–1916), had been Puerto Rico's Minister of Grace, Justice, and Government under the Island's brief autonomy with Spain in 1897 and was later elected resident commissioner in the United States. The young Muñoz Marín became an active supporter of independence and socialism for the Island. During the 1920s, he worked as a journalist and director of the San Juan-based newspaper, *La Democracia*, then went back to New York. Muñoz Marín moved permanently to Puerto Rico in 1931 and, the next year, was elected senator from the pro-independence Liberal Party.

In 1938, Muñoz Marín founded the Popular Democratic Party (PDP); he was elected president of the Senate in 1940, and, in 1948, he became the first elected governor of Puerto Rico, with 61.2 percent of the total vote. During the 1940s, he abandoned his earlier support for independence, embraced the idea of autonomy, and increasingly moved away from political nationalism to cultural nationalism. He proclaimed the Commonwealth of Puerto Rico as a "non-colonial" pact with the United States in 1952. After winning four consecutive terms, he retired from the governorship in 1964 and served as senator until 1970. When his party lost the 1976 elections, he withdrew from public life. Thousands mourned his death in 1980.

In several speeches, essays, and notes written during the 1950s, Muñoz Marín developed his own blueprint for cultural nationalism. First, he held that the nation was the "natural space" in which a people's identity could flourish in the contemporary world. Second, he believed that it was possible to assert a strong, original, and well-defined personality without resorting to political nationalism. Third, he affirmed that Puerto Rico's collective personality was compatible with Commonwealth status. Finally, he held that it was "natural" that some traits of the Island's culture would be modified in contact with the US mainland.

In 1959, Muñoz Marín delivered the Godkin lectures at Harvard University, published as *A Breakthrough from Nationalism* later that year. There he defended "Operation Serenity," his government's efforts to rescue Puerto Rico's traditional culture, as a counterpart to "Operation Bootstrap," which promoted the Island's industrialization. Operation Serenity was a shorthand for his idealistic program of cultural autonomy, which entailed the preservation of spiritual and moral values even as the Island underwent far-reaching socioeconomic changes starting in the mid-1940s. Muñoz Marín further argued that the question of political status should be disentangled from national culture. As he wrote in an undated manuscript, asserting the "personality of our people is not in any way contrary to or incompatible with their good and sincere and free association with the US."

Muñoz Marín's discourse on the Puerto Rican "personality" was a key moment in the development of cultural nationalism on the Island during the 1950s. Under his tutelage, the Commonwealth government sought to buttress its international reputation as a postcolonial arrangement. By promoting Puerto Rican culture from the new state apparatus, Muñoz Marín articulated the concerns of much of the Creole intelligentsia since the mid-nineteenth century and especially since the 1930s. Thus, many of the Island's leading writers, artists, and teachers collaborated with the Commonwealth's cultural project during the 1950s.

Who was Pedro Albizu Campos?

Pedro Albizu Campos (1891–1965) was one of the most controversial political figures in twentieth-century Puerto Rico. Born in Ponce, he earned a scholarship from the University of Vermont in 1912. The next year he transferred to Harvard University, enlisted as an officer in the US Army in 1917, and graduated from Harvard Law School in 1922. At Harvard, he cultivated close ties with Irish and Indian students committed to overthrowing the British empire. Upon his return to Puerto Rico in 1921, Albizu Campos first joined the Union Party, which backed the Island's independence, and, in 1924, became a member of the Nationalist Party, where he was immediately named vice president. He was elected party president in 1930, a post he held until his death in 1965.

Starting in the early 1930s, Albizu Campos began to call Puerto Ricans to arms to overthrow the US colonial regime. His radical and militant rhetoric drew attention from US security agencies, including the insular police and the Federal Bureau of Investigation (FBI). In 1936, he was sentenced to ten years of prison for sedition against the US government. Because of a serious illness, he was interned in a New York hospital between 1943 and 1947, when he returned to Puerto Rico. He was arrested again in 1950, after nationalists tried to assassinate President Harry S. Truman. Governor Muñoz Marín pardoned him in 1953, but he was imprisoned again the next year. After suffering a heart attack in prison in 1956, Albizu Campos was transferred to the Presbyterian Hospital in San Juan until 1964. He died five months after Governor Muñoz Marín pardoned him once again. After Albizu Campos's death, the Nationalist Party dissolved into several factions and its members joined other parties. Today, Albizu Campos's legacy continues to influence Puerto Rican politics, especially within the pro-independence movement.

Albizu Campos personified Puerto Rican resistance to US colonialism (or, as he preferred to call it, "Yankee imperialism"). Catholicism strongly influenced his worldview, especially his moral conservatism regarding gender and family relations. In particular, he proposed to rescue the cultural values of the Hispanic heritage, as they supposedly existed in Puerto Rico before 1898. Albizu Campos attempted to institute national traditions such as displaying the Puerto Rican flag, playing the national anthem, and commemorating symbolic dates. He sought to instill patriotic values among Puerto Ricans through civic rituals such as making a pilgrimage to the town of Lares as the cradle of the Puerto Rican Revolution and invoking the leaders of the nineteenth-century pro-independence movement. Albizu Campos himself became a martyr of the pro-independence movement, and many streets and schools in Puerto Rico and in the diaspora have been named after him.

How did Muñoz Marín and Albizu Campos develop different views of the Puerto Rican nation?

Muñoz Marín turned to cultural nationalism and grew increasingly opposed to Albizu Campos's political nationalism during the 1940s and 1950s. During this period, the two leaders came into direct confrontation over the best political scenario for Puerto Rico. Muñoz Marín adopted an autonomist position that sought to reconcile the Island's political and economic ties to the United States with the preservation of Puerto Rican identity or, as he preferred to call it, "personality." Muñoz Marín's populist discourse was largely a reformist alternative to the nationalist movement that emerged during the 1930s.

Meanwhile, like political nationalists around the world, Albizu Campos insisted on establishing a sovereign state to protect and preserve the Puerto Rican nation. Furthermore, he preached that armed struggle was the only viable strategy to US colonialism. While Albizu Campos appealed to a small minority of loyal militants, Muñoz Marín attracted a broader alliance between the middle and lower classes, which he lumped together under the concept of "the people."

How did the Nationalist Party operate under Albizu Campos's leadership?

Founded in 1922 as a radical offshoot of Puerto Rico's Union Party, the Nationalist Party was devoted to creating a free, sovereign, and independent republic in Puerto Rico. The Nationalist Party represented a staunch rebuttal of US political and economic control over the Island. Although its philosophy was neither socialist nor fascist, it enshrined the small independent farmer as the backbone of the Puerto Rican nation. Under Albizu Campos's leadership, the party became a militant patriotic organization, but never developed a mass following.

The Nationalist Party participated for the first and only time in electoral politics in 1932, when it only obtained 5,257 votes (1.4 percent of the total). In 1935, Albizu Campos announced that the party would withdraw from local elections. Instead, the organization adopted armed struggle as its main strategy to obtain independence. Over the next two decades, nationalists had several bloody confrontations with the insular police, especially during two massacres in Río Piedras (1935) and Ponce (1937). In 1950, the Nationalist Party led an armed revolt in Jayuya, a town in the central highlands. The last major nationalist armed event occurred in 1954 at the US House of Representatives, when four Nationalist Party members shot and wounded five Congressmen. The perpetrators of the attack—Lolita Lebrón (1919–2010), Andrés Figueroa Cordero (1924–79), Irvin Flores (1925–94), and Rafael Cancel Miranda (b. 1930)—were tried and convicted to long imprisonment sentences in federal prisons, until their release in 1978 and 1979.

How did World War II affect Puerto Rico?

The entrance of the United States into World War II in 1941 led to the expansion of military operations in Puerto Rico, considered "the Gibraltar of the Caribbean" by US security forces. The Island was transformed into a major US military enclave, designed to protect the southern border of the US mainland and the Panama Canal from enemy attacks, especially German submarines. The US government built or enlarged several army, navy, and air force bases throughout Puerto Rico, especially in San Juan, Aguadilla, Ceiba, and Vieques. Thousands of military personnel were stationed on the Island during the war.

The Puerto Rican economy received a boost in federal funds assigned to the armed forces and other defense-related agencies. These funds created thousands of jobs, expanding the federal government in Puerto Rico. Roosevelt Roads in Ceiba became the largest US naval base outside the continental United States and the main military installation in the Caribbean. Another base on the offshore island of Vieques, originally planned as a safe haven for the British fleet, was transformed into a major site for US military exercises, including a firing and testing ground for various weapons. A total of 65,034 Puerto Ricans served in the US armed forces during World War II, particularly in the Panama Canal Zone. Many were assigned to the 65th Infantry Regiment of the US Army, which saw combat in Europe, and later in the Korean War.

The end of the war accelerated political, social, and economic change in Puerto Rico, as well as in other Caribbean countries. The postwar period witnessed the decolonization of British, French, and Dutch territories in the West Indies, together with the reform of the colonial regime in Puerto Rico. US authorities allowed for more local participation in the territory's administration, as President Harry S. Truman appointed the first Puerto Rican governor, Jesús T. Piñero (1897–1952), in 1947. That same year, Puerto Ricans were authorized to choose their own governor, and in 1948 Muñoz Marín became the Island's first elected governor. Muñoz Marín later spearheaded the constitutional convention that created Commonwealth status in 1952.

After World War II, thousands of Puerto Rican veterans gained access to higher education, housing, federal employment, and health care benefits, which expanded their opportunities for upward social mobility. In particular, the GI bill buttressed student enrollment at the University of Puerto Rico by returning war veterans. Many of those stationed in US military installations remained in the mainland after the war and became part of growing immigrant communities from the Island.

How did the Popular Democratic Party dominate Puerto Rican politics between the 1940s and 1960s?

In 1940, the PDP, led by Muñoz Marín, won a majority of the seats in the Island's Senate, proclaiming that "status is not at issue." Party leaders promised instead to address Puerto Rico's pressing socioeconomic problems and campaigned against large sugar corporations as the main culprits of these problems. "Bread, Land, and Liberty" became the official slogan of the *populares*, as PDP members are known, who adopted the customary *pava* (straw hat) of the *jíbaros* as their emblem. The party built a multiclass alliance of intellectuals, professionals, merchants, manufacturers, small landowners, and rural workers, who were dissatisfied with the Island's stagnant economy. In 1944, the PDP won a resounding 64.7 percent of the votes. For the next twenty-four years, the *populares* won all elections in Puerto Rico, implementing sweeping social and economic changes—including an agrarian reform that solidified the support of small farmers. Muñoz Marín's charisma, popularity, and paternalistic relation with many of his sympathizers were key to the long hegemony of the *populares*.

In 1947, the PDP-controlled government launched Operation Bootstrap—a state-supported program of export-led industrialization—to modernize the economy and improve living standards. The notable success of this program, at least during its first two decades, buttressed electoral support for the *populares*. In 1952, the PDP negotiated the establishment of the *Estado Libre Asociado*, or Commonwealth status, for Puerto Rico, thus achieving greater autonomy from the US federal government. Under Commonwealth, industrialization proceeded apace. Vigorous rates of economic growth sustained a general climate of political stability on the Island from the mid-1940s to the late 1960s.

How did Puerto Rico industrialize its economy after World War II?

In 1947, Puerto Rico's legislative assembly approved Law 346, the Industrial Incentives Act, to promote the establishment of factories on the Island, by exempting them from local taxes for ten years. In addition, the insular government provided financial support to construct factory buildings, train workers, and secure loans. Puerto Rico's model of economic development also exploited several competitive advantages vis-à-vis the United States: low wages, an abundant labor force, a common currency (the US dollar), and free access to the US market. This state-run program, called Operation Bootstrap (or *Manos a la Obra* in Spanish), came to be known as "industrialization by invitation" because it relied on US investments in export manufacturing, lured by tax incentives. By promoting industrial labor at the expense of the agricultural sector, Operation Bootstrap imposed the death sentence on an already moribund plantation economy. The government's development strategy also encouraged further migration from rural to urban areas, where most factories were initially located, and to the United States.

What was Puerto Rico's policy toward migration?

US sociologist Clarence Senior (1903–74), who later directed the Migration Division (1951–60), first elaborated the project of organizing and supervising Puerto Rican migration. In an influential 1947 monograph, Senior proposed attaching an emigration office to the governor's executive staff and working closely with the Island's Department of Labor. Its main function would be to facilitate the recruitment of workers to the United States and Latin America, especially Venezuela. The agency would provide migrants with information about job openings, training, transportation, settlement, and insurance, as well as promote further emigration. Although Senior's plan to relocate Puerto Ricans in Latin America proved too expensive, his proposal of finding jobs for them in the United States later crystallized in the Migration Division.

Muñoz Marín, then president of the Senate (1941–48) of Puerto Rico, welcomed Senior's blueprint for planned emigration. In a 1946 memorandum, Muñoz Marín had agreed that it was "necessary to resort to emigration as a measure for the immediate relief to the problem posed by our surplus population, while we seek permanent solutions in the long run." The chief economist of the Office of Puerto Rico in Washington, DC, Donald J. O'Connor, also urged the resettlement of Puerto Ricans in the United States and other countries, such as Venezuela and the Dominican Republic. In a 1948 letter to then Governor Piñero and other Puerto Rican government officials, O'Connor argued that "migration can accomplish what economic programs on the island cannot do quickly"—that is, create jobs and sources of income, while reducing population growth. In particular, O'Connor advocated the relocation of young unmarried women as domestic workers in the United States, especially in Chicago. High-ranking members of the ruling PPD, such as Antonio Fernós-Isern (1895–1974), Teodoro Moscoso (1910–92), Rafael Picó (b. 1912), and Salvador Tió (1911–89), concurred with O'Connor's optimistic assessment. Thus began a state-supported program of large-scale migration as a safety valve for Puerto Rico's demographic and economic pressures.

On December 5, 1947, the Island's legislature passed Public Law 25, establishing Puerto Rico's migration policy and creating the Employment and Migration Bureau. According to this law, "the Government of Puerto Rico neither encourages nor discourages the migration of Puerto Rican workmen [sic] to the United States or any foreign country; but it considers its duty … to provide the proper guidance with respect to opportunities for employment and the problems of adjustment usually encountered in environments which are ethnologically alien." From its inception, the bureau (and its heirs, the Migration Division and the Department of Puerto Rican Community Affairs in the United States) sought "to follow its migrant citizens to facilitate their adjustment and adaptation in the communities in which they chose to live." The policy of "following migrant citizens," while officially "neither encourag[ing] nor discourag[ing]" their departure, paid off in the short run. The growth of the Island's labor force slowed down, as living standards rose substantially between the 1940s and 1960s. Population control was a key tenet of the PDP's development strategy throughout this period.

How did the Island's population change during the first half of the twentieth century?

Puerto Rico's inhabitants doubled from just under one million in 1899 to two million in 1950, at an average annual rate of 1.7 percent. This relatively high rate of population growth was due primarily to elevated birth rates and decreasing death rates. During the first forty years of the twentieth century, birth rates hovered around 40 live births per 1,000 inhabitants of the Island. Death rates declined swiftly in Puerto Rico during the first half of the twentieth century, from 25.3 per 1,000 inhabitants in 1899 to 8.8 per 1,000 inhabitants in 1950. As a result, many policymakers and scholars held that overpopulation—often called a "population explosion"—was one of Puerto Rico's most intractable problems.

How was Puerto Rico transformed from a predominantly rural to an urban country?

Whereas Puerto Rican cities in the nineteenth century had grown slowly, their residents multiplied quickly during the first half of the twentieth century. In 1899, the population living in places now considered cities represented 8 percent of Puerto Rico's inhabitants. By 1950, 23.3 percent of the Island's residents lived in one of the four cities then in existence. The first urban conglomerate of 50,000 inhabitants or more arose between 1910 and 1920. San Juan, the capital of Puerto Rico, which in 1910 had 48,716 inhabitants, reached 71,443 persons in 1920. Ponce became a city in a statistical sense in 1930, Mayagüez in 1940, and Río Piedras in 1950.

Between 1900 and 1930, Puerto Rico's cities began to receive a large wave of rural immigrants, particularly those displaced by a faltering coffee industry. The development of commercial agriculture, which increased import and export trade, and small manufacturing industries contributed to the rapid growth of the urban population. San Juan absorbed most of the internal migration, increasing its residents from 302,765 in 1940 to 465,741 in 1950. In 1899 the San Juan metropolitan area represented only 6.9 percent of the Island's inhabitants; by 1950 it had soared to 21.1 percent. During those years, the number of places classified as urban multiplied from 17 to 54, and the proportion of the total population residing in those places increased from 14.6 percent to 40.5 percent.

One of the key urban settlement patterns during the first half of the twentieth century was the slum or shantytown (*arrabal*). These areas concentrated poor rural immigrants squatting on public lands outside the city centers; they lacked government regulation and adequate infrastructure in the form of housing, electricity, drinking water, and sanitation facilities. Shantytown growth peaked between 1920 and 1950, particularly in the San Juan metropolitan area, especially in Santurce, Hato Rey, and Río Piedras. By 1950, almost half of Santurce's population lived in *arrabales*. The Puerto Rican government later attempted to eliminate these lower-class settlements and relocate its residents to public housing projects (known in Spanish as *caseríos* or *residenciales*). The extreme concentration of the urban poor in segregated housing areas eventually exacerbated social problems such as juvenile delinquency and drug addiction.

3

PUERTO RICO AS A US COMMONWEALTH SINCE 1952

POLITICS AND THE ECONOMY

How did Puerto Rico become a US Commonwealth?

In 1950, the US Congress passed, and President Harry S. Truman signed, Public Law 600, authorizing a convention to draft a constitution and establish a republican form of government in Puerto Rico. In a referendum held on March 3, 1952, 81.9 percent of the Island's electorate ratified the Commonwealth or Free Associated State (*Estado Libre Asociado*, in Spanish). The US Congress approved the constitution (after requiring several changes, especially in its bill of rights) on July 3 of that same year; Puerto Rico's Constitutional Convention approved it seven days later, and the new Commonwealth status was proclaimed on July 25, 1952. The next year, the United Nations removed Puerto Rico from its list of non-self-governing territories. Officially, the Island was no longer considered a US colony.

The brainchild of Luis Muñoz Marín and the Popular Democratic Party (PDP), Commonwealth was originally supposed to be a transitory, intermediate status between full independence and annexation as a state of the American union. Under this arrangement, the Island's electorate selects its own government, and its representatives pass its own laws. Puerto Rico's elected governor appoints all cabinet officials and other key members of the executive branch; the insular legislature determines the government's budget; and the judicial system amends its civil and criminal code, without federal interference—as long as such measures do not contradict the US Constitution, laws, and regulations. Commonwealth status represented a greater degree of political autonomy for Puerto Rico in local matters, such as elections, taxation, economic development, education, health, housing, culture, and language. However, the US federal government remained in control of most state affairs, including citizenship, immigration, customs, defense, currency, transportation, communications, foreign trade, and diplomacy.

To what extent did Commonwealth status recognize the sovereignty of the Puerto Rican people?

The Commonwealth formula did not substantially alter the Island's legal, political, and economic dependence on the United States. All of the regulations and articles of the federal laws that ruled relations between Puerto Rico and the United States since the 1898 Treaty of Paris remained intact. Such laws and regulations still apply to the people of Puerto Rico without their consent or control. The subordinate citizenship status of Puerto Ricans continued under Commonwealth as well. Other basic elements of US–Puerto Rico relations established before 1952 include the adoption of the US dollar as the Island's currency, US customs control, US citizenship, federal labor legislation, welfare benefits, and an elected governor.

Under Commonwealth status, Puerto Rico continued to be an "unincorporated territory" that "belonged to but was not a part of the United States." The US Congress and president could unilaterally dictate policy relating to defense, international relations, foreign trade, and investment. Congress could also revoke any insular law inconsistent with the US Constitution. Moreover, Congress or the president could apply federal regulations selectively to Puerto Rico, resulting in both concessions and revocations of special privileges. In addition, many US constitutional provisions—such as the requirement of indictment by grand jury, trial by jury in common law cases, and the right to confrontation of witnesses—were not extended to the Commonwealth.

According to Commonwealth advocates, Puerto Rico entered into a solemn "compact among equals" with the United States in 1952. US authorities and Commonwealth sympathizers have long argued that the Puerto Rican people exercised their right to self-determination. Commonwealth advocates believe that this formula can be renegotiated to correct its flaws and attain greater autonomy. However, the nature of the "compact" between Puerto Rico and the United States has been disputed from its inception. Pro-statehood and pro-independence critics contend that Commonwealth is a colonial status because of the lack of effective representation and unrestricted congressional and executive power over Puerto Rico. In recent years, the US federal government has increasingly weakened the Commonwealth's fiscal autonomy, in the wake of financial crisis. Hence, both the political and economic bases of the *Estado Libre Asociado* have wavered.

In what sense is Puerto Rico a nation?

Puerto Rico meets most of the objective and subjective criteria of conventional views of the nation—among them a shared territory, language, and history, except for sovereignty. The Island possesses many of the symbolic attributes of modern nations, including a national flag and anthem; national heroes and rituals; a national system of universities, museums, and other cultural institutions; a well-developed national tradition in literature and the visual arts; and national representation in international sports and beauty contests. For decades, the Island's intellectual elite has striven to define a national identity based on defending the Spanish language, the Hispanic heritage, and other popular customs. Most important, the vast majority of Puerto Ricans imagine themselves as distinct from

Americans as well as from other Latin American and Caribbean peoples. In a 2002 poll, 60 percent of those interviewed on the Island identified Puerto Rico as their nation; about 17 percent considered both Puerto Rico and the United States to be their nation; and only 20 percent chose the United States alone.

However, most of the Island's electorate does not currently support the creation of a sovereign state in Puerto Rico. Rather, Puerto Rican voters have reiterated an overwhelming preference for US citizenship and permanent union with the United States. A key issue is the freedom to travel to the United States under any political status option. Under the Commonwealth, Puerto Ricans have unrestricted entry into the US mainland. They would retain that right under statehood but probably lose it after independence.

How does the Commonwealth government operate?

By most accounts, Puerto Rico is a liberal democracy, characterized by free elections, multiple parties, and respect for civil liberties. Between 1952 and 2016, the Commonwealth held seventeen Island-wide elections and ten plebiscites and referenda. Only in the 2012 primaries were there any major accusations of electoral fraud. Three main political parties—the PDP, the New Progressive Party (NPP), and the Puerto Rican Independence Party (PIP)—compete for majority support and control of the insular government. Two of them, the PDP and the NPP, have alternated in power eight times between 1968 and 2016. Puerto Ricans enjoy a high degree of civil rights and political freedoms, compared to other Latin American and Caribbean countries. The Commonwealth as well as the US constitutions protect the rights to free speech, assembly, organization, religion, privacy, equal protection under the law, equal pay for equal work, and many other rights taken for granted by US citizens. In addition, the Island possesses a vigorous free press, high rates of electoral participation, and free trade unions.

However, Puerto Ricans on the Island do not enjoy all the rights and freedoms as US citizens in the mainland. Even though islanders cannot vote for the president of the United States, they are bound to follow his or her orders like any other US citizens. Because islanders do not pay federal taxes, they are not entitled to voting representation in the US Congress. Yet they qualify for most federally funded programs, although not on a par with the fifty states, including nutritional assistance, welfare, and unemployment benefits. These contradictory elements lie at the heart of the argument that Commonwealth status is a partial democracy, based upon the collective subordination of Puerto Ricans to the United States. Such an incongruence may well warrant the term "postcolonial colony" to describe the Island's unresolved status and troubled relationship with the United States.

How have Puerto Ricans responded to the Island's militarization by the United States?

As many as 200,000 Puerto Ricans have served in the US armed forces since 1917. In 2011, more than 10,000 residents of Puerto Rico were on active military duty in the US armed forces, in addition to about 24,000 persons of Puerto Rican origin living stateside. In 2015, the census estimated that 83,846 veterans lived on the Island and 220,500 Puerto Rican veterans were based in the fifty United States. The Island remains one of the leading recruiting stations for the US armed forces, especially among young members of the working classes. The military experience of so many Puerto Ricans has left a deep imprint in their daily lives—from completing their specialized education to improving their English language skills to experiencing ethnic and racial segregation.

Several sectors of the Puerto Rican population have protested against US military operations on the Island. During the Vietnam War (1965–75), opposition to compulsory military service was widespread at the University of Puerto Rico, particularly among members of the Pro-Independence University Federation (*Federación Universitaria Pro Independencia*, FUPI, founded in 1956). Another source of friction were military training programs such as the Junior Reserve Officer Training Corps (JROTC) on university campuses. Since the 1970s, various grassroots groups, from independence advocates to ecumenical coalitions, have continued to resist the Island's militarization.

Why did the pro-independence movement decline in popularity after the 1950s?

During the first half of the twentieth century, the local movement to obtain sovereignty garnered growing support, and several political parties included independence in their platforms. Since the 1960s, however, the autonomist and annexationist movements have dominated Puerto Rican politics. Meanwhile, support for independence has become a minority position. The PIP is currently the main representative of this stance, together with smaller groups that do not participate in local elections, such as the Hostosian National Independence Movement (*Movimiento Independendista Nacional Hostosiano*). In the 2012 status plebiscite, independence drew only 4 percent of the vote.

The pro-independence movement has lost electoral backing largely because it appealed mainly to an intellectual elite that viewed itself as a patriotic vanguard, but did not attract the bulk of the native ruling and working classes. Instead, independence has been primarily the political project of a radicalized sector of the middle class—including small merchants, manufacturers, independent artisans, liberal professionals, and government employees. During the 1930s, the leaders of the Nationalist Party were mainly lawyers, journalists, physicians, dentists, pharmacists, and small business owners. Even today, the pro-independence movement draws most of its membership among liberal professionals, small property owners, and other middle-class sectors. Most local entrepreneurs have not embraced independence because they identify their economic interests with continued association with the United States.

Since the mid-1970s, the massive extension of welfare benefits through transfer payments from the federal government has strengthened support for annexation to the United States. Without the allegiance of either the native bourgeoisie or the proletariat, resistance to colonialism has largely shifted from party politics to the contested terrain of culture. As a result, local intellectuals—especially college professors, writers, and artists—have played a role disproportionate to their numbers in the construction of a nationalist discourse. Here as elsewhere, the local intelligentsia has helped define and consolidate a national culture against what it perceives as a foreign invasion.

Why did the pro-statehood movement grow after the 1950s?

Compared to its political precursor, the Statehood Republican Party (SRP), the NPP more than tripled its share of the total vote for the governorship, from 12.9 percent in 1952 to 44.7 percent in 1968. Thus, the pro-statehood movement replaced the pro-independence movement as the main opposition force in Puerto Rican politics, dominated by the *populares* (1940–68). Since 1968, the NPP has gained control of the Commonwealth's governorship seven times in thirteen elections. Statehood advocates have now attained virtual parity with Commonwealth supporters.

The pro-statehood movement became a mass organization during the mid-1950s. Its support grew among the urban middle and lower classes, which expanded as a consequence of the Island's industrialization. Large sectors of the top and intermediate strata—such as managers and professionals—sympathized with annexation to the United States, to preserve their lifestyles and achieve their economic aspirations. In turn, the lower classes increasingly regarded statehood as a way to increase their access to state subsidies from the federal government. A new industrial elite, led by Luis A. Ferré, expanded the multiclass support for statehood, by linking elite interests to those of the popular sectors and by evolving from a conservative social position to a reformist ideology.

Who was Luis A. Ferré?

Luis A. Ferré (1904–2003) was the most significant leader of the pro-statehood movement in Puerto Rico during the twentieth century. Ferré began his political career in 1940, running unsuccessfully for mayor of Ponce; he also lost his bid for resident commissioner in 1948. He was a delegate to the convention that drafted the Commonwealth's Constitution (1951–52) and was later elected to the Island's House of Representatives (1953–56). In 1968, he founded the NPP and became the Commonwealth's third elected governor, initiating a bipartisan era in Puerto Rican politics. Although Ferré was not reelected as governor in 1972, he was subsequently elected Senate president (1977–80) and continued serving as senator until 1984.

Born to a wealthy family from Ponce, Ferré earned a bachelor's degree in science in 1924 and a master in mechanical engineering from the Massachusetts Institute of Technology (MIT) in 1925. He also pursued advanced piano studies at the New England Conservatory of Music in Boston. Upon returning to the Island, Ferré joined his father's business, the Porto Rico Iron Works, and afterward the Ponce Cement Company, established in 1942. Ferré eventually became chief engineer and president of the multimillion dollar Ferré Enterprises. In 1948, the Ferré family acquired the regional newspaper, El Día, and turned it into the Puerto Rican daily with the widest circulation, El Nuevo Día. In 1950, Ferré Enterprises purchased the Puerto Rican Cement and other companies from the Commonwealth government. In addition to his business activities, Ferré founded the Ponce Museum of Art in 1959.

Ferré's most enduring political legacy is his elaboration of the discourse of *estadidad jíbara* (peasant or Creole statehood), drawing on an earlier formulation from the 1940s. As a gubernatorial candidate in 1968 and later as governor, Ferré distinguished between *patria* (the fatherland) as the emotional attachment to one's birthplace, its landscape, people, language, and customs; and *nación* (the nation) as the political and legal institutions to which citizens owe loyalty. This key move allowed Ferré to posit the possibility of preserving Puerto Rico's cultural identity within a multiethnic federation, which he thought the United States embodied. In his view, Puerto Rico could retain sovereignty over language and cultural affairs as the fifty-first state of the American union. However, Congress has repeatedly rejected the proposal to maintain Spanish as the official language of Puerto Rico under statehood.

How did the Cuban Revolution affect Puerto Rico?

The 1959 triumph of the insurrection headed by Fidel Castro led to the establishment of the first socialist regime in the Americas. The Cuban Revolution further polarized the Western Hemisphere during the Cold War between the United States and the Soviet Union. For many, Puerto Rico became a model of democratic capitalist development, in opposition to Cuba's socialist experience. The breakup of diplomatic relations between the United States and Cuba in 1961, and the US trade embargo of Cuba established in 1962, created economic opportunities for Puerto Rico, such as an expanded market for US tourism and the rum industry. Furthermore, Puerto Rico was a key site of US military operations during the Cold War, especially in the offshore islands of Vieques and Culebra, as well as counterintelligence activities. Thus, Puerto Rico became a bastion of anti-Communism in the Caribbean and Latin America.

To this day, the Cuban revolutionary government has unconditionally supported Puerto Rico's independence advocates, particularly at the United Nations and the Movement of Non-Aligned Countries. Since the early 1960s, Cuban authorities established close ties with the Pro-Independence Movement (PIM or *Movimiento Pro Independencia*), created in 1959 and later transformed into the Puerto Rican Socialist Party (PSP, 1971–93). In turn, the Marxist-Leninist ideology espoused by the Cuban government increasingly radicalized pro-independence activists in Puerto Rico. Similarly, the Cuban Revolution inspired Puerto Rican militants in the United States, such as the Young Lords and the Pro-Independence Movement, during the 1960s and 1970s.

The Cuban Revolution also triggered the resettlement of more than thirty-six thousand exiles to Puerto Rico between 1959 and 2014. The exiles quickly established themselves as a "middle-man minority" in San Juan, specializing in key sectors of the Puerto Rican economy such as the mass media, professional services, retail trade, and construction. Cuban refugees tended to reinforce the conservative ideology of Puerto Rico's middle and upper classes. Some right-wing clandestine groups within the exile community, such as Alpha 66 and Omega 7, endorsed the use of violence against the Cuban government and the pro-independence movement in Puerto Rico, particularly between the 1960s and 1980s. More broadly, the presence of an influential and prosperous Cuban exile community in San Juan nurtured the fear of "another Cuba," contributed to the popular rejection of independence as a viable option for Puerto Rico, and generally supported the annexationist movement to the United States.

Why did the New Progressive Party win local elections in 1968?

In 1968, the PDP lost its first gubernatorial elections in twenty-eight years of political hegemony (1940–68) and began to alternate in power with the NPP. For its part, the recently created NPP received 10 percentage points more of the total vote (44.7) than its predecessor, the Republican Statehood Party, in 1964 (34.7). Several factors led to the electoral triumph of NPP president and candidate for the governorship, Luis A. Ferré, in 1968. First the PDP split into two factions, when Governor Roberto Sánchez Vilella (1913–97) decided to run separately for reelection, under the People's Party (PP), which won 10 percent of the votes. In turn, the PDP only received 44.7 percent of the votes, compared to 59.4 percent in 1964.

Second, the NPP campaign, based on the catchy jingle "This has to change," attracted many voters disgruntled with the *populares'* administration. The NPP built a coalition of social forces, including managers, professionals, and other members of the urban elite, as well as large numbers of the urban working and marginal classes, such as residents of public housing projects. The latter voted largely against the PDP and its municipal administrations in the San Juan metropolitan area, especially because of its urban renewal policies, including slum clearance.

Third, the NPP elaborated the discourse of *jíbaro* statehood, combining the annexationist impulse with safeguarding Puerto Rican culture. Pro-statehood leaders no longer favored cultural assimilation to the United States as a prerequisite for annexation. Instead, they claimed that US federalism would protect the Spanish language once Puerto Rico joined the American union.

Finally, the party embraced a populist program that appealed to low-income sectors of the population, especially through the expansion of federally funded programs to Puerto Rico, such as nutritional assistance, housing subsidies, and other benefits. For many poor families on the Island, statehood promised an improvement in their living standards.

Why has popular support for Commonwealth status waned since the 1960s?

The Commonwealth formula has lost ground to the pro-statehood movement as a result of several factors. To begin, the postwar transition from a rural agricultural economy to an urban industrial and service economy undercut the PDP's electoral base. Moreover, the PDP leadership repeatedly failed to enhance the Commonwealth's autonomy during the 1950s and 1960s. Since the 1970s, the downturn of the Puerto Rican economy eroded support for Commonwealth and strengthened the annexationist movement. More recently, the exhaustion of Operation Bootstrap, previously based on federal tax exemptions under Section 936 of the Internal Revenue Code, has dealt a serious blow to the Island's development strategy. Finally, the US Supreme Court has reiterated that ultimate power over Puerto Rico resides in the US Congress, thus countering pro-Commonwealth leaders' claims about autonomy.

What is the current state of Puerto Rico's status debate?

The Island has held four plebiscites about its political status since 1967. In the most recent (2012) plebiscite, 51.7 percent of the voters expressed dissatisfaction with the status quo, but none of the available options obtained a majority. Less than half (44.6 percent) expressed a preference for statehood, while nearly one-fourth (24.3 percent) supported a sovereign Commonwealth and more than a fourth (26 percent) left a blank ballot, presumably in favor of the current territorial status. Despite changing definitions of the Commonwealth formula, the plebiscites have shown a waning support for this option, down from 60.4 percent of the votes in 1967. Conversely, statehood advocates increased from 39 percent of the total in 1967 to a high of 46.5 percent in 1998 and decreased slightly in 2012. The two majority options—Commonwealth and statehood— are now in a virtual stalemate, with a small minority in favor of independence (between 3 and 5 percent of the electorate since 1993).

In June 2016, the US Supreme Court further debilitated the Commonwealth's legal claims to sovereignty and autonomy. First, it ruled that two men accused in federal courts could not be tried for the same crime in Puerto Rican courts of selling firearms. Second, it upheld the lower courts' decision that Puerto Rico could not enact its own bankruptcy law to restructure the debt of its public utilities. Hence, the Island's colonial relationship to the United States has come under increasing scrutiny, especially in the context of Puerto Rico's continuing economic crisis.

What are the major political parties on the Island today?

The main political parties in Puerto Rico are divided primarily along the lines of the three status options: Commonwealth, statehood, or independence. The PDP advocates the maintenance and improvement of Commonwealth status. The party has been closely identified with the Commonwealth formula since 1952 and its industrialization policy, Operation Bootstrap. The *populares* are ideological heirs to the autonomist movement of the late nineteenth and early twentieth centuries.

The *populares* rose to power in 1940 under Muñoz Marín's charismatic leadership and populist ideology. The party's electoral stronghold was initially located in the Island's rural areas, mainly in the inner highlands of the west and southwest, where coffee was the dominant cash crop. The PDP swept elections by more than 60 percent of the vote between 1944 and 1956, but garnered less than 50 percent after 1960. Since the 1950s, PDP leaders have unsuccessfully pressed for increased local autonomy, including greater control over foreign policy, external trade, and immigration. A faction of the *populares* has recently proposed to assert Puerto Rico's sovereignty through a compact of free association with the United States, similar to the one established with several Pacific islands. The PDP president and candidate for governor in 2016 was David Bernier (b. 1977).

In contrast, the NPP promotes Puerto Rico's full integration into the United States as the fifty-first state of the union. NPP leaders believe that federal statehood represents the culmination of permanent association with the United States and the expansion of citizenship rights. The *penepés* (as statehood supporters are locally known) argue that statehood would improve economic opportunities and guarantee equal political representation for Puerto Ricans. The NPP has supported major revisions to the economic policy of Operation Bootstrap since its founder Luis A. Ferré was elected governor in 1968. The party has traditionally drawn most of its electoral support from the urban middle and lower classes, especially in the San Juan metropolitan area. Under Carlos Romero Barceló's presidency (1974–87), the NPP lobbied for statehood as the best option for the Island's poor through the extension of US welfare programs to Puerto Rico.

The NPP has controlled the Commonwealth government seven times since 1968. Yet it has been unable to obtain a majority of the votes in any status plebiscite. Nevertheless, two NPP candidates have won the governorship with more than 50 percent of the votes: Pedro Rosselló (b. 1944) in 1996 and Luis Fortuño (b. 1960) in 2008. The NPP's gubernatorial candidate, Ricky Rosselló (b. 1979), won the elections in 2016. He is the son of former Governor Rosselló, who also served as party president between 1991 and 1999.

Gilberto Concepción de Gracia (1909–68) and other PDP dissidents founded the PIP in 1946 to create an independent, sovereign, and democratic republic in Puerto Rico. In 1952, the PIP received the second-largest number of votes on the Island after the PDP, but its electoral strength declined to less than 5 percent of the votes after 1960. PIP candidates have never won the governorship or the post of resident commissioner, but have been elected to the Island's legislature, where they have served as a political check on the two dominant parties. The party's gubernatorial candidate in 2016 was Senator María de Lourdes Santiago (b. 1959).

The insular police and the FBI surveilled, harassed, and persecuted thousands of *pipiolos* (PIP members) and other groups deemed "subversive," particularly during the heyday of the *carpetas* (secret intelligence files) between the 1950s and 1980s. The PIP underwent a period of radicalization during the 1960s, mainly as a result of the influence of the Cuban Revolution. Under Rubén Berríos's (b. 1939) presidency (since 1970), the party became more moderate and adopted a social democratic program; it is currently affiliated with the Socialist International. Although the party promotes Puerto Rico's full sovereignty, it has proposed a ten-year transition period with dual citizenship with the United States, duty-free access to the US market, and federal subsidies for social programs before decolonization. This proposal is strangely reminiscent of the idea of "free association," promulgated by some sectors of the PDP.

How serious is corruption in the Island's government and law enforcement?

Large-scale government corruption has been well documented in Puerto Rico over the last two decades. Since 1999 the local press has frequently reported on numerous cases of bribery, money laundering, and embezzlement by both of the main parties in power, the NPP and the PPD. The Commonwealth agencies with the most notorious instances of corruption have been those with the highest levels of federal funding—Education, Health, and Housing.

High-ranking officials during Pedro Rosselló's administration (1993–2001) were accused of misappropriating federal funds from grants and special contracts. In 1999–2000, several members of the board of directors of the San Juan AIDS Institute were convicted of funneling $2.2 million in federal funds for personal gain and political campaigns. In 2002, the former Secretary of Education, Víctor Fajardo-Vélez, pleaded guilty to charges of money laundering and extortion, involving a $4.3 million kickback scheme that required contractors to pay 10 percent of their contract amount. The secretary personally embezzled more than $3 million, while about $1 million ended up in NPP campaign coffers.

Between 1999 and 2002, federal prosecutors accused five NPP mayors and two PDP ones of fraud and extortion. These cases involved the misappropriation of relief funds from the Federal Emergency Management Agency (FEMA) for municipal cleanup after Hurricane Georges in 1998. The mayors were convicted of extorting from or conspiring with contractors to appropriate almost $22.6 million by billing FEMA for services not rendered.

Police corruption has been a major issue in Puerto Rico at least since the 1990s. Between 1993 and 2000, the Island's Police Department expelled about one thousand officers due to criminal charges. In 2001, thirty-two police officers were arrested for protecting cocaine shipments to the Island; between 2003 and 2007, seventy-five others were convicted of police corruption. The FBI arrested eighty-nine Puerto Rican police officers and other law enforcement officers in 2010 for aiding drug dealers. Ten more were arrested in 2015 for stealing drugs, planting evidence, and taking bribes. Not surprisingly, in 2011 the US Department of Justice characterized the level of crime and corruption involving Puerto Rico's police officers as "staggering."

According to the Drug Enforcement Administration (DEA), Colombian drug cartels use the Island as a money-laundering center. Since April 1996, the US Department of the Treasury requires banks and financial institutions to file "suspicious activities reports" (SARs) about suspected incidents of money laundering or fraud. Between 1996 and 2000, local banks and financial institutions filed 2,527 SARs. Puerto Rico ranked number thirty-three in the United States, with California, New York, Florida, and Texas leading the list with most SARs. In January 2003, Banco Popular de Puerto Rico, the Island's largest bank, paid $21.6 million in penalties to settle accusations of money laundering by the US Department of Justice.

Why did the US Navy abandon its major military bases in Vieques and Roosevelt Roads?

On April 19, 1999, private security guard David Sanes Rodríguez (b. 1954) died accidentally during a military exercise in Vieques, an offshore island-municipality of Puerto Rico that had been occupied by the US Navy since 1941. Soon after Sanes Rodríguez's death, Puerto Ricans of all ideological persuasions and walks of life called for an end to live bombings, the navy's exit, and the return of military lands to the civilian residents of Vieques.

On May 4, 2000, the US Navy carried out Operation Access to the East, removing more than two hundred peaceful demonstrators from its training grounds in Vieques. Afterward, more than 1,640 persons were arrested for trespassing on federal property, particularly during military practices. According to the head of the Puerto Rican chapter of the American Civil Liberties Union, the federal government committed multiple violations of human rights, such as using pepper spray and tear gas on unarmed protestors, and denying them due process after their arrest. Those practicing civil disobedience included a wide spectrum of political and religious leaders, university students, environmentalists, and community activists.

In June 2000, a survey conducted by the Catholic diocese of Caguas found that 88.5 percent of Puerto Rico's population supported the navy's exit from Vieques. No other issue in recent history has galvanized such a strong consensus in Puerto Rican public opinion. Despite the strong solidarity displayed by Puerto Ricans on and off the Island, the US Navy continued military exercises in Vieques. Without voting representation in Congress, islanders were forced to accept a 2000 directive by President Bill Clinton (timidly negotiated by then Governor Rosselló), which did not please most opponents of the navy's bombing of Vieques. This directive called for the resumption of military training activities, although with inert bombs, as well as for a plebiscite in Vieques. On July 29, 2001, 68.2 percent of the voting residents of Vieques supported the navy's immediate retreat from the island. International pressure, together with a strong grassroots movement, finally forced the navy to abandon Vieques on May 1, 2003. A year later, the Roosevelt Roads Naval Base—whose main function was to service the

US Navy's bombing practice and Atlantic fleet at Vieques—was closed down as well. Puerto Rico suddenly lost its role as the core of US naval operations in the Caribbean.

What are some of the leading community initiatives on the Island today?

During the early twentieth century, feminist groups in Puerto Rico struggled for equal rights in voting, education, and work. After the granting of suffrage in 1936, the feminist movement languished but reemerged during the 1970s. A second wave of women's organizations turned to issues such as sexism in education and the media, labor discrimination, health, and domestic violence. Two pioneering organizations formed during this period were Women Join Now (loosely translated from *Mujer Intégrate Ahora*, 1972) and the Confederation of Puerto Rican Women (1975).

The feminist movement was influential in passing new laws on employment discrimination (1972), family and marriage relations (1975), sexual harassment (1988), domestic violence (1989), and other issues affecting women. During the 1980s and 1990s feminists increasingly mobilized around reproductive rights, sexual orientation, and racial identities. One of the leading organizations that emerged during this period was the Coordinator of Peace for Women (*Coordinadora Paz para la Mujer*, 1989), a coalition of thirty-five groups focusing on violence against women. The coalition is still active today. Another feminist organization, the Broad Women's Movement (*Movimiento Amplio de Mujeres*), was founded in 2007, with more than twenty affiliates.

Lesbian, Gay, Bisexual, Transgendered, and Transsexual (LGBTT) activism has risen in Puerto Rico since the 1970s. The Gay Pride Community, founded in 1973, was the first gay rights organization on the Island; its main purpose was to combat discrimination against the LGBTT community through political action, educational programs, and public exposition and confrontation. In particular, it sought to eradicate antigay statutes in the Island's penal code regarding sexual acts. The Puerto Rican Lesbian and Gay Coalition, formed in 1991, and other groups representing the LGBTT community have been concerned primarily with HIV prevention, same-sex marriage, and discrimination by sexual orientation. In 2003, Pedro Julio Serrano (b. 1974) founded *Puerto Rico para Tod@s* (Puerto Rico for Everyone), a nonprofit organization that advocates for equal rights regardless of a person's sexual preferences.

Puerto Rico's student movement has traditionally revolved around the Island's political status, militarization, university autonomy, and public access to higher education. Since the 1930s, many university students mobilized in support of independence for Puerto Rico and resorted to strikes and other forms of collective protest. Between the late 1960s and early 1970s, the Island's student movement fiercely opposed the Vietnam War. After the war ended in 1975, student activism turned to more practical issues, such as the rising costs of higher education, budget cuts, and privatization. Between April and June 2010, a coalition of student organizations shut down the University of Puerto Rico system, followed by several protests between October 2010 and March 2011.

Several grassroots groups in contemporary Puerto Rico are primarily involved with environmental issues. The Island's ecological movement has grown significantly since the 1960s, especially in connection with the impact of industrialization on environmental contamination. One of the longest-standing ecological organizations is Industrial Mission of Puerto Rico, established in San Juan in 1969 and initially sponsored by the Episcopal Church. This and other groups like Casa Pueblo (founded in Adjuntas in 1980) have raised public awareness about the environmental risks of unbridled development. Among other projects, such organizations have advocated the expansion of recycling facilities and the conservation of forest areas and other natural resources, and have denounced the proliferation of urban sprawl and shopping centers.

How did Operation Bootstrap transform the Island's economy?

In the two decades after the end of World War II, Puerto Rico's rates of economic growth were among the highest in the world, averaging 5.3 percent during the 1950s and 6.8 percent during the 1960s. In the immediate postwar period, the Island offered US businesses the highest profit rates in the Americas. As a result, hundreds of US factories relocated to Puerto Rico. In 1956 the net income generated by manufacturing ($175.3 million) for the first time surpassed the share in agriculture ($162.1 million). At its peak during the 1950s, on average, one factory was set up every day. By 1958, Puerto Rico's Economic Development Administration had promoted 494 factories, employing 36,900 workers. By 1969, it had attracted 1,785 factories with 106,977 workers in Puerto Rico.

The Island's postwar industrialization led to impressive socioeconomic successes. Per capita Gross Domestic Product (GDP), measured in current dollars, practically quintupled, from $278 in 1950 to $1,353 in 1970. Less dramatically, unemployment declined from 12.9 percent in 1950 to 10.8 percent in 1970. Meanwhile, manufacturing employment grew from 55,000 workers in 1950 to 141,000 workers in 1970. Real wages, measured in 1984 prices, nearly quadrupled, from a weekly average of $41.64 in 1952 to $153.18 in 1972. The annual reports of the Puerto Rico Planning Board documented the constant growth in the local production of cement, the number of motor vehicles and telephones, and the consumption of electrical power. Such figures were widely considered indicators of economic development, along with average life expectancy and the number of teachers and physicians, which also increased significantly.

Progress in wages, employment, and living standards was directly related to the free movement of labor between the Island and the US mainland. During the 1950s, an estimated 325,000 Puerto Rican workers migrated to the United States, mostly to the East Coast. Had such mass migration not taken place, the Island's unemployment rate would have been 22.4 percent in

1960, almost double the actual rate of 13.2 percent. Exporting surplus labor thus became part of the government's economic development plans, helping to stem population growth and unemployment levels. As government planners predicted in the 1940s, migration became a survival strategy for thousands of Puerto Rican families.

For two decades, Operation Bootstrap served as a model of economic development for poorer countries in Asia, Africa, and Latin America. Thousands of foreign observers—from Haiti and Ecuador to India and Iran—visited Puerto Rico to learn firsthand about "industrialization by invitation" under the Point Four Program (created in 1950 by the Truman administration). Formerly dubbed "the Poorhouse of the Caribbean," the Island became increasingly known as a "Showcase of Democracy." The living conditions of most Puerto Ricans undoubtedly improved as a consequence of Operation Bootstrap. Whether the Island's postwar industrialization experience could be exported to other countries was a more dubious proposition.

What were the main stages of Operation Bootstrap?

Puerto Rico's industrialization program has undergone three main phases: (1) the light manufacturing/labor-intensive stage (1948–65), emphasizing the production of textiles, apparel, and leather goods; (2) the heavy manufacturing/capital-intensive stage (1965–76), based on oil refining and petrochemical industries; and (3) the high technology/high finance stage (1976–present), which has favored pharmaceutical, electric, and electronic companies. Each of these stages entailed different combinations of capital, labor, and technology, with various implications for the employment of local workers.

The first stage of Operation Bootstrap mostly attracted US manufacturing plants specializing in low-wage operations and low-capital investments, such as the garment industry. In 1950, the average hourly wage in Puerto Rico was only 28 percent of that in the United States. That same year, food products represented 48.9 percent of the net income generated by the Island's manufacturing sector, while clothing represented 18.5 percent. By 1969, the Island was the leading clothing supplier to the US mainland. However, the increasing cost of labor made manufacturing operations more expensive during the 1960s and 1970s. The US Congress gradually raised the minimum wage in Puerto Rico, thus reducing its competitive advantage as a source of cheap labor. In addition, US labor unions, such as the International Ladies Garment Workers Union (ILGWU), lobbied against the relocation of US factories to the Island, arguing that they displaced jobs from the US mainland.

The second phase of Puerto Rico's industrialization strategy turned to capital-intensive industries that paid higher salaries to skilled and semiskilled workers, and invested heavily in machinery, especially in the petrochemical industry. Government planners hoped that refining crude oil from Venezuela would generate subsidiary industries such as manufacturing oil-derived materials (synthetic fibers, fertilizers, and plastic materials). By 1970, chemical products and machinery generated 33.5 percent of Puerto Rico's net manufacturing income. However, the capital-intensive phase of Operation Bootstrap collapsed with the 1973 international oil crisis, which dealt a death blow to the Island's oil refining and petrochemical industries.

The third and current phase has relied on the intensive use of skilled labor and high technology in the manufacturing process, as well as the conversion of Puerto Rico into an international financial center. Initially spurred by Section 936 tax benefits, many US companies specializing in pharmaceuticals, electronic equipment, and scientific instruments were established on the Island. Section 936 companies had to deposit their tax-exempt revenues in Puerto Rico for at least six months before repatriation, which benefited banking institutions on the Island. The elimination of Section 936 seriously threatened this "high finance/high technology" strategy. Between 2006 and 2015, the Island's total banking assets shrank by 42 percent, from $99.1 billion to $57.3 billion.

What were the limits of Puerto Rico's model of economic development?

Although Operation Bootstrap attracted numerous factories to the Island, it was unable to slow down the swift decline of the agricultural sector. In 1940, 44.9 percent of the Island's labor force was still employed in agriculture; by 1970, only 9.8 percent was. During this period, the Island lost 162,000 agricultural jobs, while only gaining 76,000 manufacturing jobs. The scarcity of farm work expelled a large share of the rural population, both within and outside the Island. Since the 1970s, agriculture has become practically insignificant, whereas manufacturing has dominated the Puerto Rican economy.

Six decades after its creation, the Commonwealth's economic deterioration contrasts with the promise of the first two decades. The year 1974 marked the beginning of the Island's economic deceleration. Annual rates of economic growth declined to an average of 3.3 percent during the 1970s and 2.1 percent during the 1980s. Unemployment soared and wages stagnated. In addition to the lingering effects of the 1973 oil crisis and the second oil shock of 1978, the Puerto Rican economy suffered structural problems such as the growing costs of labor, transportation, and energy, which made the Island less attractive for investment. Moreover, the Puerto Rican economy was overly dependent on the United States as its main source of investment capital, consumer markets, and external finance.

How has women's socioeconomic position changed on the Island since the mid-twentieth century?

After World War II, labor-intensive manufacturing (mainly the garment, textile, leather, and food processing industries) created increasing employment opportunities for Puerto Rican women. At the same time, the home needlework industry practically disappeared with the rise of clothing factories. The garment industry offered many women their first paid jobs outside their homes. In 1950, more than 60 percent of all women in Puerto Rico employed as factory operators were textile and apparel workers. On average, female-dominated industries (such as leather and food manufacturing) paid lower salaries than male-dominated ones (such as chemical and machinery production).

The decline of labor-intensive industries in Puerto Rico since the mid-1970s reduced the share of manufacturing jobs among women, relative to other sectors of the economy. At the same time, the overall female labor force participation rate increased from 27 percent in 1975 to 34.2 percent in 1995. During this period, most employment opportunities for women emerged in white-collar occupations in the service sector, especially in public administration and retail trade. By 1980, 26.9 percent of all employed women in Puerto Rico were clerical workers; in 2015, 21.2 percent were office and administrative support workers.

Overall, women's socioeconomic status has improved in Puerto Rico since the mid-1940s. As a group, women have surpassed men in university enrollments and graduation rates. Women have become active in public life as professionals (especially teachers), writers, and politicians. They have also increased their electoral participation and representation in the insular and municipal legislatures. In 2001, Sila María Calderón (b. 1942) was elected the first female governor in Puerto Rico.

Unfortunately, gender inequality persists in many areas of social life, including occupational segregation and wage differentials between men and women. Despite their higher educational attainment, women still lag behind men in well-paid professions, such as medicine and engineering. Gender relations within the family and marriage are now more equitable than before, but many women are forced to carry a "double burden"—in addition to their customary duties as wives, mothers, and homemakers, they are often the primary bread-winners and heads of their households.

Why did Puerto Rico face an economic crisis during the 1970s?

Between 1973 and 1976, Puerto Rico's model of development confronted its first major challenge, caused by a world recession due to increasing oil prices, after the abolition of the US quota system for oil imports. In addition, the continuous increase in minimum wages made the Island less competitive vis-à-vis other newly industrializing countries, such as Mexico, Ireland, and Singapore. Many low-wage manufacturing plants closed down and moved to more attractive locations for US businesses. Real per capita income declined for the first time in the postwar era, from $1,196 in 1974 to $1,178 in 1977. The unemployment rate rose from a low of 11.6 percent in 1971 to a record high of 23.5 percent in 1983.

How did Section 936 of the US Internal Revenue Code affect manufacturing industries on the Island?

Approved by the US Congress in 1976, Section 936 allowed US corporations to operate in Puerto Rico and other US possessions without paying federal taxes. In 1983, the average profit rate for Section 936 corporations on the Island (54.1 percent) was five times higher than in the US mainland (10.3 percent). Section 936 tax benefits amounted to $2.5 billion in 1989, mainly for companies specializing in pharmaceutical products ($1.2 billion) and electrical and electronic equipment ($346 million). By 1994, tax credits under Section 936 in Puerto Rico reached $3.9 billion.

The US Congress repealed Section 936 in 1996 because it represented a huge loophole in corporate tax laws and a substantial loss in revenue to the federal government. In addition, Section 936 generated few high-paying jobs in Puerto Rico. Instead, it created an offshore financial haven for transnational corporations, many of which transferred their profits and royalties from their patents to the Island in order to claim federal tax exemption. For instance, in 1977, PepsiCo, Inc., declared 21 percent of its total global revenues in Puerto Rico. After a ten-year transition period, Section 936 was phased out completely by 2006. Efforts by Puerto Rican and US lobbyists to approve a similar program in Congress have proven unsuccessful. Operation Bootstrap had run out of steam.

How did the 1994 adoption of the North American Free Trade Agreement (NAFTA) hurt the Puerto Rican economy?

NAFTA eliminated tariff and other barriers to trade and investment among the United States, Canada, and Mexico. The treaty undermined Puerto Rico's unique status as a territory with free access to the US market. In particular, NAFTA made Mexico a major competitor to Puerto Rico in low-skilled, labor-intensive manufacturing. Average wages in Mexico were four times lower than in Puerto Rico at the time. Consequently, the Island lost thousands of factory jobs in textiles and apparel, tuna canning, leather, and agricultural products. After NAFTA, the increase in US-Mexico trade and investment induced the relocation of many of these industries from Puerto Rico to Mexico. By 2015, Puerto Rico only exported $143.7 million in textiles and apparel, compared to $877.7 million in 1993. Since NAFTA's implementation in 1994, Puerto Rico increasingly relied on Section 936 tax benefits to retain US corporations, especially pharmaceutical companies.

What is the role of federal transfer funds from the United States to Puerto Rico?

Unilateral transfer payments from the US federal government play a dominant role in the Island's economy. The introduction of the food stamps program in 1974–75 greatly increased state subsidies to Puerto Rico's lower-income families. The program began with an allocation of $388.4 million in 1975 and nearly doubled to $754.8 million the next year. By 2015, the federally funded nutritional assistance program in Puerto Rico amounted to $1.8 billion, and 39 percent of the Island's households were receiving food stamps.

Federal transfers to Puerto Rico grew astronomically, from $659.5 million in 1974 to $16.3 billion in 2015. Government programs, especially those for nutritional assistance, housing subsidies, and educational grants, have served as an extensive web of social protection on the Island. In addition, most Puerto Ricans are covered by unemployment and disability insurance, and many have earned benefits such as Social Security, Medicare, and veterans' pensions. The latter benefits have become the main form of state subsidies for Puerto Ricans with scarce economic resources.

Aside from helping meet the basic needs of the population (such as food, housing, education, and health care), federal transfer payments have discouraged employment and labor force participation in Puerto Rico. Unemployment has been an enduring problem of Puerto Rico's economy throughout the twentieth century and the beginning of the twenty-first. Despite the Island's rapid industrialization after World War II, unemployment always remained above 10 percent. Moreover, the labor force participation rate—the percentage of persons 16 years and older who are employed or searching for a job—fell from a high of 48.1 percent in 1972 to 39.9 percent in 2015, one of the lowest in the world. The inability to generate sufficient employment has been one of the main shortcomings of Puerto Rico's model of industrial development.

What is the contribution of tourism to the Island's economy?

Tourism has been a significant (but still relatively modest) sector of Puerto Rico's economy after World War II. In 1949, the government-owned Puerto Rico Industrial Development Corporation (PRIDCO) built and furnished the first modern luxury hotel in San Juan and leased it to the Hilton hospitality chain for twenty years. In 1998, Hilton purchased the property and renovated and expanded the Caribe Hilton.

The Puerto Rican Tourism Company (PRTC) was established in 1970 to promote tourism on the Island. Since the late 1970s the company has encouraged internal tourism through independently owned and operated country inns (*paradores*) outside the San Juan metropolitan area. In 2000, the Commonwealth established a Convention Center District on the former grounds of the Miramar Naval Base, attracting new investment in hotels, restaurants, and other retail activities.

By 2015, tourism represented $70.1 billion or 6.8 percent of the Island's Gross National Product (GNP), and contributed 69,519 jobs (7.1 percent of total employment). The tourist industry has been one of the few growing sectors of the Puerto Rican economy since 2006. Unfortunately, the Zika outbreak on the Island stunted the industry's growth in 2016.

With 3.5 million international tourist arrivals in 2015, Puerto Rico is the second-leading tourist destination in the Caribbean, after the Dominican Republic. That same year, San Juan also had one of the largest cruise-ship ports in the Caribbean, with 1.5 million visitors, and the busiest international airport, with 8.7 million passengers. The Island currently boasts eighty-six hotels, many of them with casinos, with more than fifteen thousand available rooms, mostly in the San Juan metropolitan area. The vast majority (98.2 percent) of the visitors come from the United States, lured by short and frequent flights from the eastern seaboard, as well as the Island's warm weather, abundant sunshine, beaches, and historic sites. Moreover, Puerto Rico uses the US dollar as its currency, and does not require US passports to travel from the fifty United States.

What were the main causes of Puerto Rico's economic recession beginning in 2006?

The Island has recently experienced the most severe and prolonged economic crisis in its modern history since the Great

Depression (1929–33). Between 2006 and 2015, Puerto Rico's economy (measured as Gross National Product at constant 1954 prices) shrank by 16.4 percent, while total employment fell by 27.4 percent. The elimination of federal tax exemptions, which undermined the Island's manufacturing base, was the basic cause of the recession. The closing down of many factories had a negative ripple effect on the Puerto Rican economy, including banking, construction, and public administration. The US recession (2007–9) aggravated the Island's economic predicament, coupled with the bursting of the "bubble" in the local real estate market beginning in 2005. In May 2006, the Commonwealth government partially shut down because of lack of funds to cover its payroll, leaving nearly one hundred thousand public employees without pay for two weeks.

Furthermore, increasing oil prices between 2005 and 2012 made it more expensive to operate businesses on the Island. The establishment of a local sales tax of 7 percent in 2006, coupled with the high cost of public utilities such as water and electricity, have reduced the disposable income of Puerto Rican households. The local sales and use tax rose to 11.5 percent in May 2015. The escalating prices of foodstuffs and gas have further reduced the purchasing power of the Island's residents. In 2016, the cost of living in the San Juan metropolitan area was 11.6 percent higher than in the fifty United States.

What factors led to the Island's public debt crisis?

Puerto Rico's sustained economic deterioration since 2006 has been associated with a spiraling cycle of public debt. The Commonwealth accumulated fiscal deficits as it continued to borrow money by issuing municipal bonds, to pay public employees and maintain public services. Instead of restructuring its economy after the demise of Section 936, the insular government more than doubled its debt from $17.6 billion in 1996 to almost $40 billion in 2006. The debt nearly doubled again to over $72 billion in 2015. Much of the Island's debt stems from public corporations such as the electrical power authority, the government development bank, the transportation authority, and the water and sewage authority. The Commonwealth government has taken austerity measures to reduce public spending and increase state revenues—such as laying off thirty thousand public employees in 2009 and cutting back state contributions to public pension systems. But such measures have been insufficient to straighten the Island's finances. In 2014, the three main credit rating agencies (Fitch, Moody's, and Standard and Poor) downgraded the Commonwealth's bonds to junk status.

On June 28, 2015, Governor Alejandro García Padilla (b. 1971) declared that "the debt is not payable." Because Puerto Rico is not a state of the American union, it does not qualify for federal bankruptcy; because it is not a sovereign country, it cannot apply for emergency financial assistance from multilateral organizations such as the International Monetary Fund. In May 2016, the Commonwealth government declared a fiscal state of emergency and a moratorium on its public debt obligations. In July 2016, the Commonwealth government defaulted on nearly one billion dollars in debt payments.

How has the US Congress proposed to address Puerto Rico's dire fiscal situation?

In June 2016, the US House of Representatives passed a bill, H.R. 5278, called PROMESA (Puerto Rico Oversight, Management, and Economic Act), to address Puerto Rico's public debt. The Senate later passed a similar bill, S. 2328, which was quickly approved by President Obama, who asserted that this was the only viable option for Puerto Rico. However, the legislation faced strong opposition in Puerto Rico, particularly from labor unions, pro-independence supporters, and some elected officials. PROMESA placed the Island's fiscal affairs under direct federal control in order to restructure its debt. On August 31, 2016, President Obama appointed a seven-member oversight board from a list of candidates nominated by Congress, including four Puerto Ricans (two Republicans and two Democrats). This board is strangely reminiscent of the Executive Council, which ruled the Island between 1900 and 1917 with little input from Puerto Rican elected officials. In any case, PROMESA will destabilize one of the pillars of Commonwealth status, fiscal autonomy from the federal government.

4

PUERTO RICO AS A US COMMONWEALTH SINCE 1952

POPULATION AND CULTURE

How did the Puerto Rican population change after World War II?

The Island's population growth rate contracted markedly during the second half of the twentieth century. This trend was mainly due to the insular government's campaigns to reduce birth rates, by encouraging family planning and emigration to the United States. From 1950 to 1980, the Island's inhabitants only increased from 2.2 million to 2.7 million, reflecting an average annual growth rate of 1.2 percent. Population growth rates increased considerably between 1960 and 1980 after reaching their lowest point during the 1950s. These rates slowed down even further over the last two decades of the twentieth century to an average of 0.9 percent annually, reaching a total of 3.8 million inhabitants in the year 2000. The number of inhabitants actually declined between 2000 and 2015.

Demographic statistics show a constant decrease in Puerto Rico's birth rate since 1950. Live births hovered around 40 per 1,000 inhabitants during the first half of the twentieth century. Between 1950 and 2010, the birth rate fell from 38.5 to 11.4. This was mostly due to the drastic decrease in the average number of children born to each woman, from 5.2 to 1.7 for the period in question. Today, the fertility rate for Puerto Rico's women approximates statistical norms for the world's highly industrialized nations (generally less than two children per woman).

Current birth rates in these countries do not ensure population replacement. The decline in birth rates has occurred much more rapidly in Puerto Rico than in Western Europe or North America.

Death rates also decreased during the twentieth century. Between 1950 and 2010, the number of deaths per 1,000 inhabitants fell from 25.3 to 7.9, after experiencing a slight increase during the 1990s. The significant drop in death rates can be credited to improvements in public health, greater access to medical services, the control of epidemic diseases, and a rising standard of living. Low death and birth rates have led to a noticeable spike in the share of aging persons within the population. By 2010, 17.4 percent of the Island's residents were 65 years or older, more than double the average for Latin America and the Caribbean as a whole (6.8 percent) and surpassing the corresponding figure (13 percent) for the United States.

Emigration from Puerto Rico intensified during the 1940s, partly due to public policies aimed at reducing population growth. Unfortunately, statistics on the flow of people between the Island and the continental United States are unreliable given the lack of official migration records. The available data do serve, however, to illustrate the major trends in Puerto Rican emigration to the United States since the mid-twentieth century. The number of people moving to the US mainland reached massive proportions in the 1940s and peaked during the 1950s. The exodus stabilized during the 1960s and 1970s, only to regain intensity in the following two decades. Today the outward flow of Puerto Ricans continues unabated.

Since 1960, immigration has had an increasing impact in Puerto Rico. Immigrant flows can be broken down by national origin as follows: (1) returning Puerto Ricans; (2) descendants of Puerto Ricans born abroad; (3) US nationals of non-Puerto Rican origin; and (4) other people born outside Puerto Rico or the United States. The first category—returning Puerto Ricans—accounts for the largest percentage of immigrants to the Island. However, the last category, notably immigration from the Dominican Republic, accelerated during the last three decades of the twentieth century.

Puerto Rico is now one of the Caribbean countries with the greatest number of residents born abroad. In 1899, only 1.6 percent of the Island's inhabitants had been born elsewhere. By 2015, 8.1 percent had been born in the United States and other countries. Nevertheless, those born outside the United States represented only 2.8 percent of the total. The vast majority were Puerto Ricans born in the United States, followed by those born in the Dominican Republic, Cuba, and, to a lesser extent, Colombia, Venezuela, Spain, Mexico, and China.

How did the Commonwealth government attempt to reduce population growth on the Island?

Since the mid-1940s, the PDP-led government tried to control the Island's population through migration and family planning. The spread of contraceptive methods, sterilization, and abortion has brought Puerto Rico's birth rate in line with more economically developed countries. This demographic phenomenon has reduced the average number of children per woman, as well as household size and the percentage of dependent minors per household. The threat of depopulation in the first two decades of the twenty-first century has replaced the predominant concern about Puerto Rico's overpopulation, salient until the 1950s. The census projects that, by 2050, the Island's inhabitants will descend to 2.984 million.

In 1937, the insular legislature authorized the distribution of birth control methods in Puerto Rico. Since the mid-1930s, the Puerto Rican government unofficially promoted female sterilization as the "permanent solution" to overpopulation. La operación ("the operation," as female sterilization is known in Puerto Rico) quickly became the preferred form of birth control. Between 1947 and 1968, the sterilization rate rose from 6.6 percent to 34.1 percent of all Puerto Rican women between

20 and 49 years of age. In 1995–96, Puerto Rico registered the highest total sterilization rate in the world (48.7 percent among married women or women in unions). In 2002, the sterilization rate reached 38.5 percent. The insular government subsidized *la operación* until 1977. Today, many women continue to use it as a "voluntary" form of family planning.

Despite the Catholic Church's condemnation of birth control, Puerto Rican women have used oral contraceptives for decades. The first large-scale trials using the hormonal contraceptive pill (Enovid) were conducted on the Island between 1956 and 1964. After the United States approved its use in 1960, the pill (known locally as *la píldora*) became a common form of birth control in Puerto Rico, especially among young, educated women in urban areas. By 1974, 20 percent of Puerto Rican women were using the pill. In 2007–8, 43.6 percent preferred oral contraceptives as their main form of birth control.

Condoms are not as widespread in Puerto Rico as other methods of family planning. Cultural barriers to condom use are rooted in the *machismo* complex, which discourages men from taking measures to prevent the risk of pregnancy or sexually transmitted diseases. In addition, men often dislike condoms because they may diminish genital sensation during sexual intercourse. In the 1950s Puerto Rican men used condoms to prevent sexually transmitted diseases, more than to avoid their primary partners' pregnancy. With the rise of the AIDS epidemic during the 1980s and the Zika outbreak since 2015, the Commonwealth government has encouraged condom use. However, in 2007–8, only 14.5 percent of Puerto Rican men were using condoms.

Abortion has been legally authorized in Puerto Rico since 1973, as a result of the US Supreme Court ruling in *Roe v. Wade*. However, numerous religious and political leaders and institutions on the Island have objected to the practice. In 2010, Puerto Rico had a relatively low abortion rate of 10.7 percent of all women of childbearing age. The moral stigma attached to abortion has induced many women to seek other family planning options, such as sterilization and oral contraceptives. The availability of birth control methods through public health clinics and private medical institutions has contributed to slowing down Puerto Rico's population growth.

Why have the Island's urban areas grown so quickly since the mid-twentieth century?

Along with migration, urbanization has been one of the most consistent trends shaping Puerto Rican society in the last decades. The Island's urban dwellers increased from slightly more than 30 percent in 1940 to nearly 94 percent in 2010. The urbanization process has been one of the most rapid and comprehensive in the world. Most of the urban growth was due to the postwar exodus from rural areas, especially from the Island's interior. For example, the number of residents of San Juan, Bayamón, Carolina, and Guaynabo increased substantially between 1940 and 1970, while rural municipalities such as Comerío, Utuado, Maricao, and Adjuntas lost population.

Beginning in 1940, the rapid deterioration of agriculture, on the one hand, and the growth of manufacturing, on the other, accelerated rural-urban migration. While urban areas grew by 85 percent between 1940 and 1960, rural areas remained stable. During the 1950s, rural emigration amounted to about 335,000 persons (25 percent of the rural population in 1950), much of it directed to the United States.

A more recent pattern has been suburbanization, whereby adjacent cities or towns become incorporated into larger metropolitan areas. Here, the dominant settlement pattern has been the sprawl of middle-class neighborhoods composed of single-family homes (known locally as *urbanizaciones*), outside urban centers. During the 1990s, the municipalities of San Juan, Ponce, and Mayagüez lost population, while neighboring areas gained population. One of the reasons why urban centers lost ground was the relocation of business and industry to suburban enclaves.

Immigrants from Cuba and the Dominican Republic have clustered in the municipality of San Juan and its outlying areas such as Carolina, Bayamón, and Guaynabo. The basic settlement pattern for Cubans was to gravitate toward middle-class neighborhoods, initially in such central districts as Hato Rey and Río Piedras, and then to disperse to areas outside San Juan, such as Isla Verde and Guaynabo. In contrast, Dominicans have tended to congregate in the poorer districts within urban centers, such as Santurce and Río Piedras. Without the mass influx of Dominicans, the municipality of San Juan would have sustained an even greater population loss between 1970 and 2010. Dominican immigrants have revitalized many inner-city neighborhoods, such as Barrio Obrero in Santurce or Capetillo in Río Piedras.

How did foreign migration to Puerto Rico increase after 1960?

The Island has received hundreds of thousands of immigrants, principally return migrants and their descendants, as well as citizens of other countries. During the 1960s, foreign-born residents increased rapidly, primarily as a consequence of Cuban and Dominican immigration. In 2015, 280,494 residents of Puerto Rico had been born abroad. Of these, 97,343 were born outside the United States, including 88,985 in Latin America; 4,453 in Europe; 2,729 in Asia; and 1,176 elsewhere.

The massive influx of Cubans and Dominicans into Puerto Rico dates from the early 1960s. Two political events marked the beginning of that period: the triumph of the Cuban Revolution in 1959 and the assassination of the Dominican dictator, Rafael Leonidas Trujillo, in 1961. Puerto Rico's swift economic growth during the 1960s attracted many foreigners, displaced by political turbulence and material difficulties in their countries of origin. Between 1960 and 2014, US immigration authorities recorded the arrival of 146,308 Dominicans, 35,610 Cubans, and 64,692 persons from other countries, for a grand total of 246,610 people admitted during this period.

This was a considerable number, given that Puerto Rico had 3.5 million inhabitants in 2014.

Cuban immigration declined sharply at the beginning of the 1980s. Although thousands of Cubans left their country during the 1980 Mariel exodus, few relocated to Puerto Rico and fewer still did so in the following years. Only 11.4 percent of the Cubans who moved to Puerto Rico arrived between 1990 and 2014. On the other hand, Dominican immigration increased substantially after 1966 (when separate statistics began to be published for that country), reaching unprecedented levels during the 1990s. More than 64 percent of the Dominicans admitted legally into Puerto Rico arrived between 1990 and 2014. In addition, many crossed the Mona Channel between the Dominican Republic and Puerto Rico illegally. In 1996, US immigration authorities estimated that 34,000 undocumented immigrants, mostly Dominicans, then lived in Puerto Rico. Though no one knows for certain how many Dominicans have entered Puerto Rico in clandestine fashion, Puerto Rico often serves as a springboard to the continental United States.

What are the main demographic characteristics of contemporary Puerto Rico?

Over the last decades, Puerto Rico's population has aged greatly. The proportion of persons under the age of fifteen has decreased, while those over the age of sixty-five have increased. This age distribution has altered the conventional pyramidal structure of the population. Whereas the younger base has shrunk, the older apex has expanded continuously.

This trend is also reflected in three other indicators: (1) the increase in the median age from 18.1 years in 1899 to 40 in 2015; (2) the decrease in the death rate from 25.3 to 9 per 1,000 inhabitants over the same period; and (3) the increase in life expectancy at birth, from 30.2 years in 1902 to 79 in 2015. These changes are closely linked to improved public health throughout the twentieth century, particularly within the last sixty years, including the control of infectious diseases and progress in health care delivery.

Census projections anticipate that the percentage of Puerto Rico's population under the age of 15 will decrease from 17.4 in 2016 to 15.1 in 2035. At the same time, those over 65 will increase from 18 to 25.8 percent. In other words, the highest growth rate over the next two decades will be among senior citizens, while the lowest growth rate will be among younger people. In this respect, as well as in other demographic trends, Puerto Rico mirrors the changes in advanced industrialized societies such as the United States, Germany, or Japan.

Over the past several decades, the gender distribution of Puerto Rico's population has shifted. At the beginning of the twentieth century, the Island had a slight excess in the number of females over males. This proportion was later reversed. In 1940, the ratio of males per 100 females was 100.8; by 2015, it had dropped to 91.2. Gender imbalance is particularly noticeable among the elderly, who are predominantly female. In 2015, 56.7 percent of the Island's residents over 65 years old were women.

Mass emigration contributed to reducing the percentage of the Island's males, especially during the 1950s, when most migrants were men. Thousands of Puerto Ricans, primarily men, have also left the Island to enlist in the US armed forces. Other reasons for the decreasing proportion of males include an increased life expectancy for women, the impact of violent crime among men, and a greater incidence among men of such life-threatening conditions as heart disease and AIDS.

Why has the Puerto Rican population decreased since the year 2000?

The Island's population, which had been growing at least since the late 1700s, began to fall in 2004. For the first time in its modern history, the inhabitants of Puerto Rico decreased by 2.2 percent (82,821 persons)—from 3.808 million in 2000 to 3.725 million in 2010. The population further declined by 6.8 percent (251,975 persons) to 3.474 million between 2010 and 2015. This remarkable population loss can be attributed to three main demographic factors, linked to the Island's lingering economic crisis. First, net migration from Puerto Rico to the United States reached 311,198 persons during the first decade of the twenty-first century and 295,718 only between 2010 and 2015. Second, Puerto Rico experienced declining fertility rates—from 15.6 live births per 1,000 persons in 2000 to 9.8 live births per 1,000 persons in 2015. Finally, decreasing numbers of return migrants and foreign immigrants, especially from the Dominican Republic, have slowed down population growth.

Puerto Rico's demographic losses are partly due to a declining rate of natural increase (the difference between births and deaths, calculated at just 0.20 in 2016). In addition, the persistent economic recession on the Island has accelerated outmigration. The current migration wave (approximately 263,000 between 2010 and 2014) may well have surpassed the peak years of the "Great Migration" (approximately 237,000 between 1950 and 1954). On average, 53,020 people left the Island per year between 2010 and 2014, compared to 47,400 people between 1950 and 1954. In 2015, the number of people moving from Puerto Rico to the United States reached a record high—approximately 89,000, according to census estimates.

How do Puerto Ricans on the Island define themselves racially?

Spanish censuses show that Puerto Ricans were about evenly divided between whites and nonwhites until the mid-nineteenth century. From 1860 until the end of the twentieth century, the proportion of the Island's inhabitants classified as white increased constantly, except for the year 1899, when the first US census registered a small decrease. Census statistics for Puerto Rico show a steady rise in the percentage of people classified as white between 1899 and 1950 and, again, in 2000. (The local census dropped the race question between 1960 and 1990.) Although "racial" categories changed several times during this period, the "white" category remained intact and the proportion of persons identifying themselves as such rose from one census to the next, except in 2010. In turn, the share of the population classified as nonwhite (including black and mixed race) decreased from 38.2 percent in 1899 to 19.5 percent in 2000 and then increased again to 24.2 percent in 2010.

According to these statistics, Puerto Rico's population became "whiter" throughout the twentieth century, mainly during the first half of that century. In the 2000 census, 80.5 percent of the Island's residents described themselves as white, with only 8 percent black and 11.5 percent other races. In 2010, the proportion of whites decreased to 75.8 percent and the proportion of blacks increased to 12.4 percent, while other race categories increased slightly to 11.7 percent of the total. The reasons for the long-term "whitening" of the Puerto Rican population are too complex to be adequately dealt with here, but it is likely that many people of mixed race prefer to identify themselves as "white" rather than "black" in the census. Moreover, the multiplicity of racial terms commonly used in Puerto Rico (more than twenty) makes it difficult for many people to classify themselves according to US categories such as African American, American Indian, or Asian American. In any event, the available statistics suggest that the vast majority of people currently living in Puerto Rico perceive themselves as white.

Why is the crime rate so high on the Island?

For decades, Puerto Rico has experienced extraordinarily high rates of violent crime. Between 1990 and 1999, the Island averaged 850 murders per year. Between 2000 and 2009, the figure dropped to 774 per year. However, the Island recorded the highest number of murders in its history in 2011 (1,136). Although this figure declined to 681 in 2014, Puerto Rico still had a higher violent crime rate than other US jurisdictions. According to the FBI's Uniform Crime Reporting Program, the state with the highest murder rate in 2014 was Louisiana, with 10.7 murders per 100,000 inhabitants. No other state had a rate of 10 or more. Puerto Rico's murder rate was 19.2 per 100,000 inhabitants, surpassing the District of Columbia, with 15.2 murders per 100,000 inhabitants. Murder rates were even higher in the San Juan metropolitan area, which recorded the highest figure in the United States in 2014 (23.5 murders per 100,000 inhabitants).

One of the major reasons for Puerto Rico's high crime rate has been the increase in drug trafficking and drug addiction since the 1970s. Because of its geographic location and easy access to the United States, the Island is a major transshipment point for illegal drugs, as well as a major consumer of such drugs, especially cocaine, heroin, and marijuana. According to the Drug Enforcement Administration (DEA), Puerto Rico, with the third busiest seaport in North America and the fourteenth in the world in 1997, had become the main transit area in the Caribbean for smuggling Colombian cocaine and heroin into the United States. In the year 2000, Puerto Rico's Police Department intervened in 1,200 "drug points" (*puntos de droga*), where illegal drugs are sold. The DEA estimated in 2015 that between 20 and 30 percent of all cocaine entering Puerto Rico was consumed locally. Many of the Island's murders are related to drug trafficking, especially to gang wars for turf, in addition to longstanding problems such as poverty, unemployment, and social inequality.

How has the Zika virus affected Puerto Rico?

In 2016, a Zika outbreak aggravated the Island's prolonged economic recession. Discovered in Uganda in 1947, the Zika virus became epidemic in Brazil and other tropical countries in 2014. The virus is transmitted by the *Aedes aegypti* mosquito, which is very common in Puerto Rico and other places with warm climates, dense neighborhoods, and stagnant water. The Centers for Disease Control and Prevention (CDC) in Atlanta have identified Puerto Rico as a major focus of infection with the Zika virus and placed the Island under a travel alert, thus discouraging tourism. As of October 27, 2016, Puerto Rico's Department of Health confirmed 33,455 cases on the Island, including 2,615 pregnant women, since the first case was reported in December 2015. Five deaths and one case of microcephaly—a rare neurological birth defect—due to the Zika virus have been recorded on the Island. In addition, sixty-two persons had contracted Guillain-Barré Syndrome (GBS), which causes muscle weakness and sometimes temporary paralysis. The CDC also estimated that 25 percent of Puerto Rico's 3.5 million residents could be infected with Zika by the end of 2016.

The Zika outbreak has strained Puerto Rico's public health system, particularly aerial spraying programs to combat mosquitos. Such programs have been reduced because of budget cuts of nearly $70 million to the Commonwealth's Department of Health between 2014 and 2016. In addition, the virus has caused an overload of patients seeking treatment in health care centers throughout the Island.

In 2016, Democratic and Republican members of the US Congress debated the assignment of emergency funds to prevent the Zika virus. On July 11, 2016, six US Congressmen wrote to President Obama to express their concern about the spread of the Zika virus and the need to facilitate aerial spraying in Puerto Rico. At the same time, hundreds of citizens on the Island—including farmers, physicians, and ecologists—protested against fumigating with a pesticide (Naled), with potential toxic effects on human health. On July 22, Governor Alejandro García Padilla decided not to use Naled in the struggle against Zika on the Island. On August 12, the US

Department of Health and Human Services declared a state of health emergency in Puerto Rico, allowing additional federal funds and personnel to combat the virus. On September 28, Congress finally allocated $1.9 billion to fight the spread of Zika, including $66 million for health care for people affected by the virus in Puerto Rico and other US territories.

How has the United States influenced Puerto Rican culture?

No other Latin American country, except perhaps Mexico, has sustained such an intense contact with US culture as Puerto Rico. Aside from language, education, and religion, discussed elsewhere in this book, the United States has left a deep imprint on recreation and sports in Puerto Rico. Since the early twentieth century, official parades have commemorated US holidays such as the Fourth of July, while families have gathered for Thanksgiving dinner and children have adopted Halloween costumes. US card games such as bridge and poker were added to favorite Spanish pastimes like *brisca*. Traditional Spanish forms of leisure such as horseracing and cockfighting, organized around gambling, were considered inappropriate for young children, while modern physical education was incorporated into the public school curriculum. Movie theaters specialized in Hollywood films and jukeboxes disseminated US music recordings. The advent of radio (in 1937) and television broadcasting (in 1954) boosted the consumer market for US media and advertising. Growing access to cable television since the 1980s and the Internet since the 1990s has widened the repertoire of US and global media on the Island.

Perhaps the most evident US influence in Puerto Rico can be appreciated in sports such as baseball, basketball, and boxing. These three sports became an integral part of the Island's popular culture during the first half of the twentieth century. Local schools and universities established amateur teams and competed with each other before World War I. A semi-professional baseball league with six teams was formed during the 1930s.

Many Puerto Ricans have played baseball professionally in the US Major Leagues since 1942, including Roberto Clemente (1934–72), Orlando Cepeda (b. 1937), Jorge Posada (b. 1971), Iván Rodríguez (b. 1971), and Carlos Delgado (b. 1972).

US soldiers introduced boxing to the Island as part of their physical training soon after the Spanish-Cuban-American War. Puerto Ricans have shown increasing enthusiasm for prize fighting, especially after several of their compatriots became world boxing champions since the 1930s. Among these were Sixto Escobar (1913–79), Wilfredo Gómez (b. 1959), Félix "Tito" Trinidad (b. 1973), and Miguel Cotto (b. 1980).

More recently, basketball has attracted the largest number of players and spectators on the Island. The sport's popularity increased with the expansion of live television broadcasts during the 1970s. A handful of Puerto Ricans have played professionally in the National Basketball Association, including José "Piculín" Ortiz (b. 1963), Carlos Arroyo (b. 1979), José Juan Barea (b. 1984), and Peter John Ramos (b. 1985). Undoubtedly, the sports imported from the United States have become widely accepted in Puerto Rico.

Today, Puerto Ricans constantly cross over in a creative blending of cultural repertoires of various origins. The polar opposition between Spanish and English has given way to various degrees of bilingualism and the much-misunderstood practice of code-switching ("Spanglish") in Puerto Rican communities throughout the United States and back on the Island. The rhythms of salsa, *merengue*, rock, reggae, rap, and *reggaetón* have merged imperceptibly in people's musical tastes. The spiritual battle between Santa Claus and the Three Wise Men has given way to a peaceful coexistence between the two icons, at least in commercial terms. Protestantism is no longer an alien importation from the United States, nor entirely antagonistic to the Island's popular culture. US fast-food chain restaurants have adapted to local preferences by adding items such as *arroz con habichuelas* (rice and beans) and *tostones* (fried plantains) to their menus.

How did the Commonwealth government attempt to preserve and promote Puerto Rican culture?

Cultural nationalism became the ideology of the *Estado Libre Asociado* during the 1950s. The Commonwealth's first legislative acts in 1952 were to proclaim the national flag and anthem as official symbols of the Island, and a coat of arms quickly followed. The flag and anthem date back to the nineteenth-century pro-independence movement against Spain, while the coat of arms was inspired by a 1511 coat of arms granted to the Island by the Spanish Crown.

The Institute of Puerto Rican Culture, established in 1955, consolidated the project of defining, promoting, and defending national identity. Under its founding director, Ricardo Alegría (1921–2011), the institute sponsored a multi-pronged program of public activities, including establishing archives, libraries, museums, and parks; promoting historical, archaeological, and folkloric research; commemorating historical events and patriotic leaders; conserving colonial buildings and erecting monuments; and supporting the plastic arts, folk music, and arts and crafts. A cadre of scholars, writers, and artists codified the values, symbols, rituals, and practices that would represent the Puerto Rican nation to itself and to the world. One of their master metaphors was the organic image of the three "roots" of the Island's national identity—Taíno, Spanish, and African.

Following Alegría's conceptualization, the institute's official seal graphically encoded the ethnic/racial triad of Puerto Rican culture. The seal depicts a well-dressed Spaniard in the center with a grammar book in his hand and three Catholic crosses in the background; to his right stands a seminude Taíno with a *cemí* and a corn plant, and to his left, a bare-chested African holds a machete and a drum, with a *vejigante* (Carnival) mask lying at his feet and a sugarcane plant on one side. This visual representation has multiple symbolic connotations, among them the suggestion that the main contribution of African slaves in Puerto Rico was less cultural than economic—that is, their labor power as cane cutters. The image also suggests that Catholicism was one of the foundations of Puerto Rican culture, represented by the lamb (associated with Jesus Christ) directly underneath the Spanish man. In principle, the three figures are on an equal footing, thus evoking the myth of the harmonious integration among races and cultures.

In practice, the institute assigned different priorities to each of the three roots. Most of the institute's programs focused on the conservation, restoration, and promotion of the Island's Hispanic heritage, particularly in architecture, history, painting, popular arts, folk music, theater, and poetry. Perhaps its most notable achievement has been the preservation and recuperation of the Spanish colonial district of Old San Juan as part of the Island's national patrimony. A secondary focus of the institute has been the excavation, collection, and display of pre-Columbian artifacts, discovered through archaeological research. Unfortunately, the "third root" of Puerto Rican culture—the African one—has not received as much official attention as the first two, the Taíno and the Spanish.

How did the Spanish language become a key symbol of cultural identity on the Island?

After more than a century of US hegemony, Spanish remains the primary means of communication in Puerto Rico. Since 1949, public school instruction, as well as college education, has been chiefly in Spanish, although English continues to be a required subject from elementary schools to universities. The Commonwealth's establishment in 1952 consolidated Spanish as the main language of government and particularly of public education. The two official languages are Spanish and English. But bilingualism is limited to a small minority, mainly composed of the middle and upper classes, return migrants and their descendants, and other immigrants from the United States.

Puerto Rico remains a mostly Spanish-speaking society, with a high degree of linguistic uniformity, despite some regional and class differences. According to the 2010 census, 95.7 percent of the Island's residents spoke Spanish at home, while 4.1 percent spoke only English. Moreover, 66.4 percent reported speaking little or no English. Between 2000 and 2010, the proportion of people aged five or over who could speak English dropped by almost 9 percentage points, possibly as a result of outmigration. The vast majority of the Island's inhabitants communicate regularly in Spanish, at home, work, and school; and resort to English only occasionally for professional, commercial, or educational purposes.

The better-educated and higher-income groups tend to be bilingual. Their speech patterns approximate standard versions of both languages as taught in schools and universities. Spoken language strongly marks the distinction between rural and urban dwellers, and being called a *jíbaro* can be a great stigma, similar to "country bumpkin" in the United States. Among second-generation immigrants in the United States, Spanish dominance is receding rapidly. However, some are more fluent in Spanish than English, and others alternate between the two languages. Today, Puerto Ricans display a broad range of language practices—from Spanish monolingualism (primarily on the Island) to English monolingualism (primarily in the US mainland), including various degrees of bilingualism.

During the twentieth century, Puerto Rican nationalists embraced the Spanish vernacular as the dominant symbol of their culture. Contrary to nineteenth-century Latin America, the Spanish language is now a crucial element in Puerto Rican nationalism, partly as a reaction to the ill-fated attempt by the US colonial government to impose English as the official language of instruction until the mid-twentieth century. Nowadays, critics often equate Puerto Rican nationalism with "Hispanophilia"—the cult of all things Spanish—or at least with a preference for the Hispanic legacy, usually at the expense of the African sources.

How did cultural nationalism gain strength, while political nationalism weakened on the Island?

Whereas nationalist politics have declined in popularity, public expressions of cultural identity remain rooted in a nationalist discourse. The strong Hispanic orientation of the intellectual elite of the 1930s has been institutionalized in the Department of Hispanic Studies at the University of Puerto Rico, the Institute of Puerto Rican Culture, and the Puerto Rican Athenaeum, among other cultural sites. Assimilation into US culture has become an electoral drawback for all political parties, including the NPP. In particular, conserving the Spanish language has become a non-negotiable item under any political status option for Puerto Rico. As former NPP Governor Luis A. Ferré once explained, Puerto Rico remains the fatherland (*la patria*) while the United States is the nation (*la nación*) for the annexationist movement. For others, the Puerto Rican nation and the fatherland are one and the same, but they are divorced from a non-sovereign state that depends on the federal government (as represented by the possession of a US passport and a limited set of citizenship rights).

How have contemporary writers and artists approached Puerto Rico's national identity?

Most Puerto Rican writers and artists since the 1930s have sought to define, assert, and defend a distinctive national culture, despite the Island's political and economic dependence on the United States. The majority has contributed to a nationalist canon characterized by a nostalgic view of the past prior to 1898—particularly of the Taíno heritage—a romantic idealization of the tropical landscape, and a glorification of Hispanic customs. Most twentieth- and twenty-first-century literary anthologies, as well as school and university curricula and syllabi, have abided by the nationalist canon and enshrined the Spanish language as its cornerstone. In effect, Puerto Rican intellectuals have created a nation without a state.

For decades, the Island's literary establishment sought to defend Puerto Ricanness against the relentless onslaught of Americanization. Most canonized authors have been affiliated with the pro-independence movement and have regarded their work as a constant affirmation of the dignity of the Puerto Rican people. As the writer Edgardo Rodríguez Juliá has noted, the problem of national identity has become an obsession for many authors, concerned with questions of individual and collective memory.

Postwar Puerto Rican literature includes at least three generations of writers. The Generation of 1950 featured well-known male authors such as René Marqués (1919–79), José Luis González (1926–96), Pedro Juan Soto (1928–2002), and Emilio Díaz Valcárcel (1929–2015). These writers chronicled the traumas of postwar Puerto Rico, particularly the cultural dislocations produced by an emerging urban industrial society, as well as among Puerto Ricans in New York.

The Generation of 1970 includes Luis Rafael Sánchez (b. 1936), Rosario Ferré (1938–2016), Ana Lydia Vega (b. 1946), Magali García Ramis (b. 1946), Edgardo Rodríguez Juliá (b. 1946), and Mayra Montero (b. 1952). Their novels and short stories often challenged the dominant narratives of national identity through a revisionist historical perspective, parodic humor, an urban plebeian language, and the treatment of erotic themes. This generation of writers also incorporated the voices of previously excluded subjects, such as women, blacks, homosexuals, and migrants. Several members of this group are still active today.

Finally, the Generation of 1980—including authors such as Eduardo Lalo (b. 1960), Mayra Santos Febres (b. 1966), and Angel Lozada (b. 1968)—is no longer as compelled to address the question of Puerto Ricanness as past generations. Instead, younger writers are more interested in exploring other issues, such as gender, sexuality, race, migration, and globalization. Much of their work can be characterized as postnational, since it is less obsessed with national identity than the work of earlier writers.

How do ordinary Puerto Ricans express their national identity, despite being US citizens?

Most Puerto Ricans value their US citizenship, the freedom of movement that it allows, and "permanent union" with the United States. At the same time, Puerto Ricans of all political ideologies, not just independence supporters, define and express their cultural identities in intensely nationalistic terms. Today, Puerto Ricans perform their identities through various means, including observing holidays and participating in multiple rituals, such as parades, festivals, beauty pageants, religious processions, and informal gatherings.

One of the most important holidays is Christmas, with a special emphasis on Three Kings Day (January 6). Puerto Ricans usually commemorate Christmas with members of the extended family and consume traditional dishes, such as *lechón asao* (roasted pig), *pasteles* (green banana and meat patties), and *arroz con gandules* (rice with pigeon peas); and drink, especially *coquito* (a rum-based coconut eggnog). Music and dance usually accompany these activities. A festive spirit is a central element of Puerto Rican culture.

The Christmas season in Puerto Rico may well be one of the longest in the world. It begins the day after Thanksgiving (on Black Friday, as it is commonly known in the United States) and ends officially with the *octavitas*, eight days after Epiphany (January 6), and unofficially on Candlemas (February 2, forty days after Christmas), when Christmas trees are traditionally burned. Some would include the Feasts of Saint Sebastian in late January in an extended Christmas cycle. Such celebrations form part of the Island's Catholic and Hispanic legacy, integrated more or less seamlessly with Anglo-Saxon, Protestant traditions from the United States. Although Christmas retains its religious significance for many Puerto Ricans, it is also a common way to indulge in the pleasures of social life.

Certain types of food and dietary habits are closely identified with Puerto Rican culture. Rice, beans, cassava, plantains, sweet potatoes, pork, and salted codfish have long been part of the local diet. Islanders have consumed large quantities of some of these foods since Spanish colonial times, mostly imported from abroad. Today, many town festivals commemorate traditional foodstuffs, such as breadfruit (Humacao), land crab (Maunabo), roast pig (Las Piedras), pigeon pea (Las Piedras), plantain (Dorado), and cassava (Coamo). Puerto Rican cuisine blends ingredients from diverse origins, including indigenous, Spanish, African, and US influences. A standard cooking procedure is to prepare *sofrito*, a mixture of herbs and spices such as sautéed onion, garlic, pepper, and cilantro, as a basis for countless meals such as stews, soups, and meat dishes. Many specialties, such as *cuchifritos* (fried pork cubes), *bacalaítos* (codfish fritters), or *tostones* (fried green plantains) have a high cholesterol and carbohydrate content.

Why do most Puerto Ricans support the Island's separate representation in international sports events and beauty contests?

Puerto Rico began to participate with an independent sports delegation at the Central American and Caribbean Games in Havana in 1930. The International Olympic Committee first recognized the Island as a separate country at the 1948 Olympic Games in London. This situation is due to the concept of "sports sovereignty," referring to the autonomy of some dependent territories, like Puerto Rico, in athletic competitions. Eleven nations that are not sovereign states currently participate in the Olympics. Since 1952, Puerto Ricans have carried their own flag in international sports contests and have played their anthem when one of their athletes wins a gold medal. Despite their dependence on the United States, Puerto Ricans have claimed a place among the nations of the world through athletic diplomacy.

Today, many ordinary citizens identify with their athletic delegates in regional and world competitions such as the Central American and Caribbean, Pan-American, and Olympic Games. Regardless of their political ideology, Puerto Ricans often rejoice when one of their teams beats the United States, especially in basketball and baseball. One of the most memorable moments in Puerto Rico's Olympic history occurred in Athens in 2004, when the Island's basketball team defeated the "Dream Team" of professional players from the United States. Since 1948, the Island's athletes have won nine Olympic medals. At the 2016 Olympics in Rio de Janeiro, tennis player Mónica Puig (b. 1993) became the first delegate of Puerto Rico to win a gold medal, as well as the first woman representing the Island to earn a medal in any event. Even supporters of Puerto Rico's incorporation as the fifty-first state of the American union have advocated preserving the Island's sports sovereignty. For many islanders, Olympic participation demonstrates that they constitute a nation, despite their colonial ties with the United States.

Similarly, many Puerto Ricans follow closely the performance of their representatives in international beauty pageants. The Island has participated as a separate country in the Miss Universe contest since its inception in 1952. Many Puerto Ricans are especially proud that five women from the Island have won the title of Miss Universe: Marisol Malaret (b. 1949), Deborah Carthy-Deu (b. 1960), Dayanara Torres (b. 1974), Denise Quiñones (b. 1980), and Zuleyka Rivera (b. 1987). This figure makes Puerto Rico the third most successful country in the Miss Universe contest, after Venezuela and the United States. In 1970, Malaret's selection as the first Puerto Rican Miss Universe helped make participation in international beauty pageants an important banner of national identity. The Island has hosted the Miss Universe pageant on three occasions since 1972, with financial support from the Commonwealth government. In addition, Wilnelia Merced (b. 1957) was crowned Miss World in 1975, followed by Stephanie Del Valle (b. 1996) in 2016.

In these beauty contests, the Island competes on equal terms with numerous countries, from small dependent territories to world powers like the United States. Each time a local representative reaches the contest's finalists, her success provokes multiple expressions of joy, as well as well-attended receptions in Puerto Rico. In 2001, the nearly simultaneous victories of Denise Quiñones as Miss Universe and Félix "Tito" Trinidad as world boxing champion unleashed a wave of national pride among islanders affiliated to all political parties.

What are the most popular genres in Puerto Rican music today?

In the 1970s, salsa emerged as the leading musical expression on the Island and in the diaspora. Since then, this musical genre has reached millions of people in Latin America, the United States, and other parts of the world. Musically, the catch-all term "salsa" ranges from traditional Afro-Caribbean styles to avant-garde Latin jazz. The term "salsa" itself is a commercial label that refers loosely to contemporary Latin dance music. Literally, salsa means "sauce," but figuratively it means "soul," similar to its common use among African Americans. Salsa could be heard as a descriptive label for Afro-Latin music since the 1950s. But the current use of the term became widespread in the 1970s to market various genres from the Cuban *son* and *guaguancó* to the Puerto Rican *plena* and *bomba*, themselves composed of diverse subtypes.

Most salsa shares several musical elements. First, salsa has a fixed rhythmic time-line, the *clave*, usually 2/3 or 3/2 over two beats, generally played on two hardwood sticks, also called *claves*. Second, salsa features improvisation in both melody and harmony, in instruments as well as voices. Third, most salsa songs have a call-and-response structure, based on the alternation between the soloist and the chorus. Last, salsa contains a strong polyrhythmic organization, especially through interlocking drumming patterns, as well as the percussive use of the bass and piano.

The main pattern for salsa music is the Cuban *son montuno*. Its formal arrangement is a fixed choral scheme and features the improvisation of the singer within a basic motif. As in the *son*, salsa lyrics often employ the Spanish *copla*. Both use the *tres* or *cuatro*, the two Creole versions of the guitar, extensively. These are not exclusively Cuban elements, however. For instance, the *plena* is also performed in call-and-response fashion, and the *cuatro* is a cornerstone of the *seis* musical style.

Like much of the music heard in the Caribbean, salsa results from the fusion of African and Hispanic sources. The African heritage is evidenced in the preponderant part that the rhythmic aspect plays in all salsa. The very term "salsa" hints that percussion, and especially drumming, is central to this type of music. Above all, this is music to be danced to: a song that does not make you move your feet does not have any "salsa." The call-and-response structure prevalent in salsa can also be traced to West African sources.

Most salsa songs, written and performed in Spanish, follow Spanish rhetorical forms such as the *copla* or the *romance*. The Hispanic legacy is present in certain recurring themes: unrequited love; criminal intrigue; the figure of the *mora encantada* (the femme fatale, usually a mulatta); the picaresque underworld of thieves, pimps, and petty gangsters; the *cuadro de costumbres*, or the colorful local event. As in Spanish folk poetry, the topic of romantic love predominates in many variants: the *requiebro* or the *galanteo*, the *desengaño* and the *despecho*. Salsa lyrics often preserve sixteenth-century language patterns as well as folk wisdom in the form of proverbs and tales.

Reggaetón emerged as a commercial musical genre toward the end of the 1990s and later became the favorite dance among teenagers on the Island and other Caribbean countries like the

Dominican Republic and Cuba. Among the multiple musical influences on *reggaetón*, Jamaican reggae, especially dancehall, stands out, as well as reggae in Spanish, particularly in its Panamanian form; African American and Nuyorican hip hop; and various musical styles from the Hispanic Caribbean, such as *bomba, plena,* salsa, *merengue, bachata,* and *cumbia.*

Musically, the most distinctive element of *reggaetón* is its rhythmic formula, based on a 3/2 beat known as *dembow*, inherited from dancehall (which can be glossed as "boom-ch-boom-chick"). Furthermore, the genre often employs a style of spoken declamation over recorded songs, similar to hip hop. Much of the instrumentation is electronic and relies increasingly on digital technologies. Socially, *reggaetón* is closely associated with the subaltern classes in urban areas of the Hispanic Caribbean and the United States, such as San Juan, Santo Domingo, Havana, Panama City, New York, and Miami. Some song lyrics openly assert blackness and criticize the ideology of white hegemony; most often they celebrate a pan-ethnic *Latinidad.* The most problematic aspect of *reggaetón* is its large dose of verbal violence, particularly aimed at women. Some critics also object to the doggie-style dance, *perreo,* that usually accompanies *reggaetón*, because of its explicit sexual overtones. René Pérez (b. 1978) of the famous Calle 13 duo and Tego Calderón (b. 1972) are among the most intriguing composers and performers of this genre, sometimes repackaged as "urban music."

Why have many Puerto Ricans converted to Protestantism?

The Island is one of the Latin American countries with the highest share of Protestants, with 33 percent of the population, according to a 2014 survey by the Pew Research Center. Within the Caribbean region, only the non-Hispanic countries have a higher percentage of Protestants than Puerto Rico. This fact is surprising in a country where Catholicism was the only official religion for nearly four centuries.

Protestant denominations have increasingly attracted Puerto Ricans since the early twentieth century. Despite the presence of Protestant churches on the Island before 1898, the rise of Protestantism dates primarily from the US occupation of Puerto Rico and US efforts to "civilize" the Island. In 1899, Protestant congregations—Presbyterians, Baptists, Congregationists, and Methodists—divided the Island into four regions to facilitate their missionary work. Other denominations later arrived on the Island, such as the Pentecostals in 1916, which expanded greatly since the 1930s; various forms of revivalism; and home-grown churches such as the Congregation of Mita (founded in San Juan in 1940). By 1950, informed sources estimated that 46,629 Puerto Ricans belonged to a Protestant congregation.

Early twentieth-century missionaries sought to "regenerate" Puerto Rican culture with "progressive" ideas and habits, such as the prohibition of alcohol, to form the Protestant character of Puerto Ricans. The first Protestant ministers showed a frank disdain for local customs, such as the cult of the saints, patron saints' festivals, religious processions, and cockfighting, which they associated with an oppressive colonial state (Spain) and an equally despotic church (Roman Catholicism). In particular, they interpreted the cult of the saints as a form of idolatry. Over time, Protestant churches incorporated some Puerto Rican customs, such as musical practices.

The conversion of Puerto Ricans to Protestantism, especially to Pentecostalism, has been relentless since World War II. Thousands of islanders, dissatisfied with the Catholic Church, initially turned to the Presbyterian, Pentecostal, and Adventist churches. Among the causes of their conversion were the incentives to read the Gospel, the sense of belonging to a spiritual community, the active participation in religious ceremonies, the extensive system of health care, and the spiritual healing practices sponsored by evangelical churches. Moreover, most Puerto Rican converts have witnessed a divine healing, speaking in tongues, and prophesying as tokens of the presence of the Holy Spirit in their lives.

For many, Pentecostalism filled a spiritual void created by the Island's swift socioeconomic transformation during the twentieth century. Religious conversion often encouraged the improvement of an individual's social position, through values such as saving and austerity, the postponement of pleasure, and dedication to work.

Over the last few decades, Protestant churches have become deeply rooted in Puerto Rico. By the mid-twentieth century, most Protestant pastors and ministers were born on the Island. The emotional, spontaneous, and informal character of some evangelical rituals, especially Pentecostal ones, has drawn many faithful. The effective incorporation of lay people in the daily activities of their congregations was also an attractive feature of Protestantism. Similarly, the catchy songs, the convenience of marriage ceremonies for divorced people, and the educational and social services helped spread the Protestant message throughout the Island. A work ethic celebrating personal progress and material prosperity as signs of salvation has had a broad appeal. Finally, the financial support, extensive organization, and missionary campaigns from US churches contributed to the success of Protestant evangelizing in Puerto Rico.

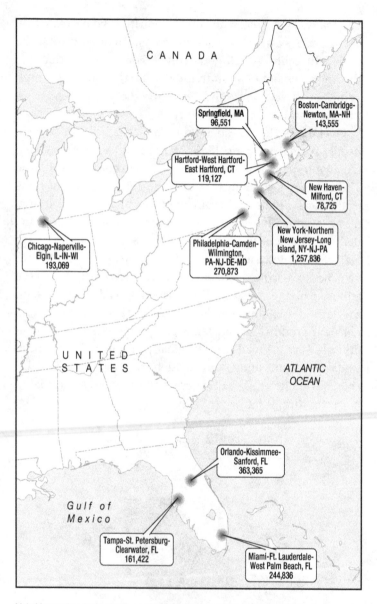

Main Metropolitan Areas with Puerto Rican Residents in the United States, 2015

5

THE PUERTO RICAN DIASPORA TO THE UNITED STATES

HISTORY, DEMOGRAPHY, AND THE ECONOMY

Who were some of the most prominent Puerto Ricans who moved to the United States during the late nineteenth century?

Several political exiles from Puerto Rico sought refuge abroad, mainly in New York City, after the failure of the Grito de Lares, the Island's insurrection against Spanish colonialism in 1868. Among them were expatriate intellectuals such as Eugenio María de Hostos, Ramón Emeterio Betances, Segundo Ruiz Belvis, Lola Rodríguez de Tió, Sotero Figueroa (1851–1923), and Arturo Alfonso Schomburg. These exiles set the stage for a much larger labor migration from Puerto Rico to the United States throughout the twentieth century.

Who was Arturo Alfonso Schomburg?

Arturo Alfonso Schomburg (1874–1938) was a leading Afro-Puerto Rican collector, bibliophile, curator, writer, and activist. Born in Puerto Rico to a laundress from the Danish Virgin Islands and a merchant of German descent, he grew up in San Juan but moved to New York City in 1891. There Schomburg immediately became involved with the Cuban and Puerto Rican independence movements. He cofounded the revolutionary club *Las Dos Antillas* (The Two Antilles), serving as secretary between 1892 and 1896. He also joined the Spanish-speaking Masonic Lodge *Sol de Cuba* (The Sun of Cuba) No. 38, renamed Prince Hall in 1911, when Schomburg became Master of the Lodge and more English-speaking blacks joined the group. He rose to leadership positions within New York's black masonic movement, serving as Grand Secretary between 1918 and 1926.

Throughout his life, Schomburg negotiated his multiple identities as Puerto Rican, West Indian, Caribbean, Spanish, black, and American. After the end of the Spanish-Cuban-American War of 1898, he gradually withdrew from Puerto Rican and Cuban affairs and turned increasingly to the African American community. During the 1920s, Schomburg collaborated with the intellectual leaders of the Harlem Renaissance, including W. E. B. Dubois, Langston Hughes, and Claude McKay. He also published frequently on African American topics in the English-language press of New York, using the pen name Guarionex (alluding to a Taíno *cacique*).

Schomburg assembled one of the largest collections of historical materials on the African diaspora of his time, including rare books, manuscripts, letters, pamphlets, artwork, and other artifacts. He sold more than 10,000 items to the Harlem branch of the New York Public Library in 1926 and later became the curator of his own collection until his death. His materials form the core of the Schomburg Center for Research on Black Culture, one of the preeminent archives on the African diaspora in the Americas.

What were the main destinations of Puerto Rican migrant workers during the first half of the twentieth century?

The US occupation of the Island facilitated the relocation of Puerto Ricans to other Caribbean and Pacific territories under US hegemony. Between 1898 and 1930, at least 31,000 Puerto Ricans moved to Cuba, the Dominican Republic, Hawaii, and the US Virgin Islands, particularly St. Croix. Beginning in 1900, the first major migrant stream of Puerto Ricans under US rule was directed to Hawaii, mostly recruited to cut sugar cane. Until 1910 Hawaii had the highest concentration of Puerto Rican migrants (3,510) of any US jurisdiction. Smaller settlements appeared in California and Arizona, along the travel routes to Hawaii. Others relocated across the US mainland, especially after 1917, when Congress granted US citizenship to Puerto Ricans. Hundreds worked in mainland military bases and industries. Smaller groups built railroads in Ecuador, cut cane in Mexico, grew coffee in Colombia, and worked in a clothing factory in Venezuela. A few thousand picked cotton in Arizona during the 1920s. Thousands went back to the Island during the Great Depression of the 1930s.

The largest mainland Puerto Rican settlements emerged in New York City, the US seaport with the best transportation and trade links with San Juan and with abundant employment opportunities in manufacturing and services. By 1920, New York's Puerto Rican population (7,719) was three times larger than that of Hawaii (2,581). Until the 1940s, most Puerto Ricans traveled on steamships such as the *Marine Tiger*, the *Borinquen*, and the *Coamo*. About 71,000 moved from the Island to the US mainland between 1900 and 1944.

During the first two decades of the twentieth century, thousands of skilled Puerto Rican workers, especially cigar makers, arrived in New York City. Among them were labor leaders Bernardo Vega (1885–1965), Jesús Colón (1901–74), and Joaquín Colón (1896–1964), and anarchist and feminist Luisa Capetillo. Between 1917 and 1944, Puerto Ricans clustered in working-class neighborhoods such as Chelsea, East Harlem, the Lower East Side and West Side of Manhattan, and the Brooklyn Navy Yard. These compact settlements (or *colonias*, as they were called then) contained other Spanish-speaking groups, mostly Cubans and Spaniards, and were racially diverse. By the 1920s Puerto Ricans concentrated in East Harlem, especially between East 96th and 125th Streets, which quickly became known as Spanish Harlem, or simply El Barrio, as the historic center of the diaspora. In the 1930s about 22 percent of the city's Puerto Ricans lived in El Barrio.

How did US authorities treat Puerto Rican immigrants between 1898 and 1917?

During this period, Puerto Ricans were technically "nationals" of the United States. A "national" was a person who owed allegiance to a state and was entitled to protection from that state, but was not a citizen with full civil and constitutional rights. This ambiguous legal status allowed for the recognition, under the Foraker Act of 1900, of a "Porto Rican citizenship." However, the latter status was practically meaningless outside the US legal regime, because citizenship and nationality are linked in international law, and Puerto Rico has never been a sovereign nation.

In 1902, Isabela González (1882–1971), a young, unwed, pregnant Puerto Rican woman, arrived on a steamboat in New York City and was detained in Ellis Island. Because she was considered an alien "likely to become a public charge," US immigration authorities did not admit her to the United States. However, she claimed she was a US citizen and had the right to remain in this country. She was eventually allowed to stay in New York under the care of relatives. She later decided to sue the US government, specifically the Commissioner of Immigration, William Williams. She initially lost her case in the US Circuit Court for the Southern District of New York, but then she appealed to the US Supreme Court.

In *Gonzales v. Williams* (1904), the US Supreme Court ruled that although the inhabitants of Puerto Rico were not US citizens, they were not "alien" for immigration purposes and could not be denied entry into the United States. Since then, Puerto Ricans have moved freely between the Island and the US mainland. The 1917 extension of US citizenship to all residents of Puerto Rico facilitated migration to the United States.

However, the question of whether Puerto Ricans have a separate nationality from US citizenship has been disputed for decades. In 1996, Puerto Rico's Supreme Court ruled that Puerto Rican citizenship coexisted with US citizenship. But two years later, the US State Department determined that, under current federal laws, Puerto Rican nationality could not be claimed apart from US citizenship. That same year, the US District Court for the District of Columbia reiterated that Puerto Ricans were part of the United States for the purposes of the Immigration and Nationality Act.

What was the role of the Puerto Rican government in organizing migration?

During the 1940s and 1950s, the insular government sponsored emigration as a "safety valve" to alleviate Puerto Rico's socio-economic problems. Notwithstanding its lack of sovereignty, the government acted as a "transnational" intermediary for its migrant citizens for most of the twentieth century. The insular government set up several agencies in the United States under different guises: the Bureau of Employment and Identification (1930–48), the Office of Information for Puerto Rico (1945–49), the Migration Division of the Department of Labor (1948–89), and the Department of Puerto Rican Community Affairs in the United States (1989–93).

Among other initiatives, these agencies issued identification cards for Puerto Ricans as US citizens; supervised an extensive program for contract farmworkers; promoted employment opportunities for Puerto Ricans in the United States; lobbied for the rights of migrant workers; negotiated cheap airfares between the Island and the US mainland; registered thousands of Puerto Ricans to vote in the United States; helped organize overseas Puerto Rican communities; and fostered Puerto Rican culture in the mainland. In short, the Commonwealth government instituted a transnational migration policy after 1952.

Despite (or perhaps because of) their colonial condition, Puerto Rican migrants have preserved various types of political links with their homeland. For decades, the Island's political parties have had a formal presence in the United States. The Popular Democratic Party (PDP), which controlled the insular government between 1941 and 1968, crafted the Migration Division as an informal "consulate" to further the Commonwealth's interests. When the New Progressive Party (NPP) gained power in 1969 and again in 1977 and 1985, it restructured the agency to advance the Island's annexation into the United States. In 1993, NPP Governor Pedro Rosselló and other pro-statehood leaders, then a majority in the insular legislature, abolished the Department of Puerto Rican Community Affairs in the United States. They believed that the agency represented an unwarranted instance of applying public policy in another jurisdiction. The Puerto Rico Federal Affairs Administration (PRFAA) then replaced the Department of Puerto Rican Community Affairs in the United States. Nowadays, this agency has greatly reduced its budget and influence over the diaspora.

Why did Puerto Rican migration to the United States take off after World War II?

Insufficient jobs on the Island, combined with a growing demand for cheap labor on the US mainland, sparked the first exodus during the mid-1940s. Net migration between the Island and the US mainland peaked at more than 650,000 persons between 1945 and 1964, which became known as the period of the "Great Migration." By this time, most Puerto Ricans arrived in New York City in commercial airplanes, making them the first large-scale airborne migration in history.

Most of the migrants were unskilled rural workers, with little education and knowledge of the English language, and were largely incorporated into the lower rungs of the US labor market. Thousands found jobs in seasonal agriculture, manufacturing, domestic service, and other service industries. The Island's agricultural economy, particularly in sugar, coffee, and tobacco, had plummeted since the Great Depression of 1929–33. After World War II, the government's industrialization program, Operation Bootstrap, displaced thousands of rural workers to urban areas. Especially hard-hit was the central mountainous region, including the coffee-growing municipalities of Utuado, Lares, Jayuya, and Maricao, which suffered large population losses.

What was the Puerto Rican farmworker program?

On May 9, 1947, the Puerto Rican government created the Farm Labor Program through Law 89. The main purpose of this law was to regulate the recruitment of workers in Puerto Rico and to make the Island's Commissioner of Labor responsible for this process. In 1948, nearly 5,000 Puerto Ricans traveled to the US mainland under the Farm Labor Program. In 1951, the Wagner-Peyser Act, which established the Bureau of Employment Security within the US Department of Labor, was extended to Puerto Rico. Thereafter, the federal government recognized the Island as part of the domestic labor supply in the United States. In effect, US officials treated Puerto Rico as a state of the union concerning seasonal agricultural workers. Henceforth, the Island's Farm Labor Program processed thousands of interstate clearance orders from mainland employers requesting farmworkers through the US Department of Labor.

Between 1948 and 1990, the Farm Labor Program recruited 421,238 Puerto Ricans to work in the US mainland. At the program's peak during the 1960s, an average of 17,600 workers traveled to the mainland each year. This was the second-largest organized movement of temporary laborers in the United States, after the Mexican *Bracero* program (1942–64) in the Southwest. Indeed, the negotiations between the Mexican and US governments served as a model for Puerto Rico's Migration Division. These agreements included recruitment, transportation, housing, wages, food, working conditions, hours, savings funds, and repatriation of agricultural laborers.

Although Puerto Rican farmworkers traveled to many states, they concentrated in the Northeast, especially in New Jersey, Connecticut, New York, Delaware, Massachusetts, and Pennsylvania. The vast majority were young, male, landless rural laborers in the sugar, coffee, and tobacco industries on the Island. They were commonly known as *los tomateros* (the tomato pickers), because that was one of the main crops they harvested in the United States. They also planted and cut shade tobacco in the Connecticut River Valley; picked corn, blueberries, asparagus, broccoli, and onions in the Delaware River Valley; strawberries, cabbages, and carrots in New York; apples in New England and Washington; potatoes in Maine; peaches in South Carolina; avocadoes and lettuce in South Florida; and other crops like cranberries, oranges, and mushrooms in various places. Several migrant communities originated as former contract workers resettled in cities such as Philadelphia, Lancaster, Camden, Buffalo, Hartford, Boston, Milwaukee, Detroit, and Miami.

Where did most Puerto Rican migrants settle until the 1970s?

The Puerto Rican diaspora has historically concentrated in urban areas, mainly in New York City and other northeastern cities of the United States. Many Puerto Rican communities in New York City developed alongside African American neighborhoods such as Harlem in Manhattan or Bedford-Stuyvesant in Brooklyn. In the last decades of the twentieth century, predominantly Puerto Rican *barrios* became more mixed with other Hispanics, particularly Dominicans and Mexicans. Although New York City continues to have the largest number of Puerto Ricans (695,253 in 2015), it no longer dominates the diaspora as it did decades ago.

From New York, Puerto Ricans expanded to New Jersey, Connecticut, and Pennsylvania. A Puerto Rican nucleus emerged around Philadelphia, Camden, Lancaster, and other cities along the Delaware River Valley. A secondary concentration developed in the Midwest during the 1950s, particularly in Chicago, Cleveland, and smaller industrial cities such as Lorain, Ohio, and Gary, Indiana. During the 1970s, more Puerto Ricans began to move to the South, principally to Orlando, Florida.

Contemporary Puerto Rican settlement patterns are part of a broader movement from urban centers to suburban areas, and from the Northeast and Midwest to the South and West of the United States. The Puerto Rican population has recently experienced an extraordinary growth in cities such as Orlando, Tampa, and Miami, while it has stagnated in traditional centers of the diaspora, such as New York, Philadelphia, and Chicago. The extraordinary increase in the number of Puerto Ricans in Florida contrasts with their sluggish growth in New York, New Jersey, Illinois, and Ohio.

Why were many Puerto Ricans segregated in inner-city neighborhoods?

The national origin, lower-class status, and racial diversity of Puerto Rican migrants tended to restrict their housing options. Postwar Puerto Rican communities in New York City spread across the Harlem and East Rivers into the South Bronx and South Brooklyn, transforming neighborhoods such as Williamsburg and Sunset Park. Most of the immigrants settled in dilapidated inner-city housing areas abandoned by other ethnic groups such as the Irish, Italians, and Jews. During the 1950s Puerto Ricans became the second-largest minority in New York City, after African Americans; the second-largest Hispanic population in the United States, after Mexicans; and one of the most disadvantaged groups, together with American Indians and, later, Dominicans.

Today, Puerto Ricans are still more likely than other Hispanics (except perhaps Dominicans) to live in overcrowded and deteriorated housing areas. In 2015, Puerto Ricans had one of the lowest rates (36.1 percent) of home ownership in the United States. This characteristic is related to high levels of poverty, unemployment, and concentration in central cities. Puerto Ricans in Los Angeles and Tampa are more likely to live in suburban middle-class areas than in Chicago or Hartford. Overall, the degree of residential segregation of Puerto Ricans from non-Hispanic whites and blacks decreased between 1990 and 2010.

How have Puerto Ricans in the United States defined themselves racially?

According to census reports, the racial composition of Puerto Ricans in the United States changed substantially from 1940 to 2010. First, the percentage of stateside Puerto Ricans classified as white decreased drastically since 1980, largely as a result of the inclusion of a new Hispanic category in the census. In 2010, the proportion of Puerto Ricans who described themselves as white (53.1 percent) was much lower than in 1940 (86.8 percent). Second, the proportion of black Puerto Ricans has remained extremely low since 1950 (between 4 and 8.7 percent). Third, those reporting other races (aside from American Indian, Asian, and Hawaiian and other Pacific Islander) jumped from less than 2 percent in 1970 to 36.5 percent in 2010. Thus, over the past three decades, Puerto Ricans in the United States have shifted their racial self-perception from a predominantly white population to a multiracial one. Contrary to the dominant trend on the Island, fewer of those residing stateside reported that they were white between the 1970 and 2010 censuses.

These figures suggest that Puerto Rican immigrants and their descendants do not fit well in the rigid white/black dichotomy that still dominates race relations in the United States. To begin, Puerto Ricans use more racial terms than most Americans, including *trigueño* (literally, wheat-colored), *moreno* (dark-skinned), *indio* (Indian), *quemao* (tan), *jabao* (light-skinned with visible Negroid features), and *grifo* (dark-skinned with "kinky" hair). Moreover, the Puerto Rican folk system of racial classification insists on a person's physical appearance, often downplaying her ancestry. Finally, Puerto Ricans have a long history of interracial unions since the Spanish colonial period. Puerto Ricans do not automatically consider the offspring of such unions as black; instead, they place them along a racial continuum defined by skin pigmentation, hair texture, and nose and lip form.

Why did many Puerto Ricans return to the Island in the 1970s?

A restless circulation of people (or "revolving-door migration") has characterized the Puerto Rican exodus, especially between 1965 and 1980. In several years, more Puerto Ricans went back to the Island than left for the US mainland, particularly as a result of minimum-wage hikes on the Island and the fiscal crisis of New York City, the historic core of the Puerto Rican diaspora. During the 1970s, net migration to the mainland reached its lowest point (less than 76,200) since World War II. At the same time, about 267,000 Puerto Ricans returned to live on the Island. Among the main causes of the reverse flow were declining living conditions and employment opportunities in New York City, Chicago, and Philadelphia. In addition, a warmer climate, strong family ties, the Spanish language, and a Hispanic cultural environment drew many Puerto Ricans back home.

Consequently, the movement of first- and second-generation Puerto Ricans to the Island took massive proportions. The 1980 census found that 6.2 percent of the Island's population was born in the fifty United States, mostly of Puerto Rican parents. The presence of hundreds of thousands of Puerto Ricans raised in the United States and speaking English as their first language raised critical issues about the Island's cultural identity, notably the role of the Spanish language as a symbol of that identity.

Islanders dub return migrants and their children "Nuyoricans," an epithet that originally referred to Puerto Ricans in New York City. As currently used in Puerto Rico, Nuyorican encompasses all Puerto Ricans born, raised, or living in the United States. The term often implies that Nuyoricans are somehow less Puerto Rican than those who remained on the Island. The Nuyorican stereotype highlights the migrants' alleged Americanization, including their way of speaking, dressing, walking, and relating to others. Island-born Puerto Ricans often perceive Nuyoricans as a different group, and Nuyoricans also tend to distinguish themselves from both Island-born Puerto Ricans and Americans. Typically, islanders deem Nuyoricans as more aggressive, disrespectful, and promiscuous than themselves. In turn, Nuyoricans perceive themselves as more cosmopolitan and sophisticated than islanders.

Why did large-scale emigration resurge after the 1980s?

High emigration rates from the Island resumed largely because of the persistent wage discrepancy between Puerto Rico and the United States. In 1989, islanders earned on average less than half as much as their US counterparts. The gap was much higher in some occupations, such as police officers, construction workers, electricians, nurses, and physicians. Furthermore, precarious socioeconomic conditions—especially high poverty and unemployment rates—continued to plague the Island. Beginning in 1996, the phaseout of Section 936 wreaked havoc in Puerto Rico. In 1999, poverty levels on the Island (48.2 percent) were nearly quadruple those in the fifty United States (12.4 percent). Puerto Rico's unemployment rate (19.2 percent) was almost triple that of the United States (5.8 percent) in 2000. Trying to escape such economic woes, nearly a quarter of a million Puerto Ricans moved to the US mainland between 1980 and 2000.

How has the geographic distribution of Puerto Ricans in the United States changed over time?

The settlement patterns of Puerto Rican migrants have shifted greatly over the last five decades. Although Puerto Ricans still cluster in the state of New York, their proportion decreased from nearly three-fourths of the total in 1960 to about one-fifth in 2015. For the first time ever, the number of persons of Puerto Rican descent in New York declined (albeit slightly) during the 1990s. Still, New York has the largest concentration of Puerto Rican residents of any state. Meanwhile, the proportion of Puerto Ricans has grown elsewhere, above all in Florida. The states with the largest increases in their Puerto Rican population include Pennsylvania, Massachusetts, Connecticut, and Texas.

The current stage of the exodus may be called "post-Nuyorican" because many Puerto Ricans have moved away from the New York metropolitan area, especially to Central and South Florida. As the diaspora has become more scattered, regional differences have intensified. For instance, Puerto Ricans tend to be financially better off in the Southeast and Southwest than those in the Northeast and Midwest. Moreover, Puerto Ricans are more likely to encounter Cubans in Miami and Mexicans in Los Angeles than either group in New York City, where they are more prone to interact with African Americans and Dominicans. Contemporary Puerto Rican migration is much more dispersed throughout the United States than in the past.

How and why have Puerto Ricans moved to Florida?

The modern history of the Puerto Rican exodus to Florida dates back to the late nineteenth century. The earliest wave of Puerto

Rican migrants, from about 1885 to 1940, settled primarily in the Tampa Bay area, mainly in Ybor City, the core of the US cigar-making industry. Hillsborough County was the hub of Florida's small Puerto Rican population until 1930. Between 1940 and 1980, most Puerto Rican migrants shifted to South Florida, especially to Miami, which provided job opportunities in seasonal agriculture, the garment industry, and tourism. Long before the emergence of Orlando as a major migrant destination, Miami's Dade County recorded 17,329 Puerto Rican residents in 1970 and 44,656 in 1980. Since the 1980s, most Puerto Ricans have moved to Central Florida, mostly to the Orlando area. They included veterans who had been stationed in Florida's numerous military bases and engineers recruited by NASA's Kennedy Space Center in nearby Cape Canaveral.

The first large-scale movement of Puerto Ricans to Florida took place under the Farm Labor Program sponsored by the Migration Division of Puerto Rico's Department of Labor. Hundreds settled in South Florida during the 1950s, especially in Dade, Broward, and Palm Beach Counties. Most were seasonal workers specializing in the harvesting and processing of vegetables, such as potatoes, beans, avocados, corn, tomatoes, and lettuce. During the summer, many traveled north to work in farms and returned south during the winter.

The Puerto Rican exodus to Central Florida began in earnest in the late 1960s, when hundreds of islanders acquired properties near Orlando, particularly in Deltona, in Volusia County. Many bought land and houses with the intention of retiring in the area. During that period, Spanish-language advertisements in the Island's newspapers began to market cheap lots in Central Florida. The 1971 opening of Walt Disney's first theme park in Orlando spurred real estate speculation in the region, and middle-class islanders saw a lucrative investment opportunity there. The earliest wave of immigrants consisted primarily of retired persons looking for a quieter and safer lifestyle in Central Florida. Later, the migration stream to Florida encompassed Puerto Ricans from New York, New

Jersey, and Illinois. By 1980, the census counted 6,662 residents of Puerto Rican descent in Orange County, which includes the city of Orlando, while nearby Seminole County had 2,079 and Osceola 417.

Puerto Rican migration from both the Island and the US mainland surged in the mid-1980s. By then, compact Puerto Rican enclaves had emerged in several counties of Central Florida, mainly Orange and Osceola. The small city of Kissimmee, about twenty miles south of Orlando, became increasingly Puerto Rican. Thousands moved to new suburban communities such as Meadow Parks in Orange County and Buenaventura Lakes in Osceola, both developed by Landstar Homes. New migrants had an easier time finding temporary housing with established relatives, following their leads into potential job opportunities, and visiting local stores that sold Puerto Rican products and food.

In the 1990s, the city of Orlando experienced the largest increase (142 percent) in the number of Puerto Ricans stateside. During that decade, Orange and Osceola Counties displaced the Bronx as the leading destinations for Puerto Rican immigrants. By 2004, Orlando was the second largest metropolitan area for Puerto Ricans in the United States, after New York. Today, Greater Orlando houses a larger Puerto Rican population (363,365) than such well-established centers of the diaspora as Philadelphia and Chicago. During the first two decades of the twenty-first century, Central Florida and especially the Orlando-Kissimmee-Sanford metropolitan area witnessed the greatest expansion of the stateside Puerto Rican population.

Why are stateside Puerto Ricans increasingly marrying outside their ethnic group?

Puerto Ricans have a much higher intermarriage rate than other Latinos in the United States. In 2009, 45.2 percent of all stateside Puerto Ricans were married to non–Puerto Ricans, mainly non-Hispanic whites (23.1 percent) and other Latinos (15.3 percent).

Few Puerto Ricans (3.8 percent) were married to non-Hispanic blacks. US-born Puerto Ricans and those who have lived longer in the United States are more likely to marry outside their group than those born on the Island and those who have migrated recently. The growing intermarriage rate may lead to the consolidation of a pan-ethnic identity, such as Hispanic or Latino, or even a new multiracial category. In any event, marriage data suggest that Puerto Ricans are establishing close ties with other ethnic and racial groups in the United States.

How has emigration affected the Island's economy?

The main economic effect of the Puerto Rican diaspora was to temporarily slow down the growth of the Island's labor force after World War II. Exporting surplus labor became an integral part of *Manos a la Obra* or Operation Bootstrap. Ironically, as the sociologist Frank Bonilla once put it, the state-run program of industrialization could have been named *Manos que Sobran* (literally, "Idle Hands"), given the massive dislocation of agricultural workers. As government planners predicted during the 1940s, moving from rural to urban centers, and from the Island to the US mainland, became a survival strategy for hundreds of thousands of people.

The diaspora's economic significance can be partially gauged through the migrants' monetary transfers to their relatives back home. Between 1947 and 1958, Puerto Rican farmworkers sent approximately $292 million to the Island. Puerto Rico's balance of payments shows the steady expansion of private remittances over the last five decades, especially during the 1990s. Although much smaller than in neighboring countries such as the Dominican Republic, remittances to Puerto Rico increased nearly eleven-fold between 1970 and 2005, from $57 million to a high of nearly $621 million, and then declined to $430 million in 2015. Together with transfer payments from the US government, remittances are a basic asset for low-income households on the Island.

More recently, the continuing exodus has represented a net loss of economic resources on the Island. In 2014, for instance, the relocation of 68,099 Puerto Ricans to the United States meant that they did not pay an estimated $86 million in taxes to the Island's government. In addition, those migrants did not consume foodstuffs, electricity, water, fuel, and other basic items on the Island, thus contributing to a diminution of local economic activity. Overall, current outmigration rates are associated with high costs for the Puerto Rican economy, despite some economic gains such as remittances.

Why have Puerto Ricans remained one of the most disadvantaged ethnic minorities in the United States?

In the 1920s and 1930s, stateside Puerto Ricans concentrated in lower-status occupations such as laundry workers, dishwashers, porters, janitors, garment workers, waiters, and domestic employees. During the 1940s and 1950s, most Puerto Rican immigrants lacked the educational credentials, occupational experience, and English-language skills required for white-collar jobs. By 1960, Puerto Ricans in New York were predominantly unskilled workers, such as machine operators, laborers, and packers. Nowadays, Puerto Ricans in the United States are more likely than other ethnic and racial groups to be blue-collar and service workers, except private household workers.

Puerto Ricans still constitute one of the most underprivileged groups in the United States. Most socioeconomic indicators place them in the lowest rungs of the US social structure, below non-Hispanic whites, Asians, and other Hispanics such as Mexicans and Cubans. The only other minority group with a similarly distressed socioeconomic profile are African Americans. According to recent census data, Puerto Ricans are more likely to be unemployed and poor, to live in female-headed households, and to have lower levels of income, educational attainment, and occupational status than most major ethnic and racial groups. For instance, Puerto Ricans had a median household income of \$40,774 in 2015, compared to \$55,755 for the entire US population, \$59,698 for non-Hispanic whites, \$44,782 for all Hispanics, and \$36,544 for non-Hispanic blacks. In 2012, Puerto Ricans owned only 7.8 percent of all Hispanic-owned businesses in the United States, even though they represented 9.4 percent of the Hispanic population.

Such figures document the persistent material deprivation of stateside Puerto Ricans, seven decades after the takeoff of mass migration. Their deteriorating living conditions since the 1970s were largely due to the deindustrialization of New York City, Philadelphia, Chicago, Boston, and other cities, as well as the increasing polarization between well-paid skilled jobs and low-paid unskilled jobs, particularly in the service sector. The automation, computerization, suburbanization, overseas relocation, and decline of manufacturing sectors like the garment industry displaced many Puerto Rican workers, who were heavily concentrated in such sectors.

The Great Recession of 2007–9 disproportionately affected the socioeconomic status of Puerto Ricans in the United States. Their unemployment rate jumped from 9.9 percent in 2007 to 16 percent in 2011, while their poverty rate grew from 24.3 percent to 27.4 percent during the same period. Despite the US economic recovery since 2011, Puerto Ricans continue to encounter major barriers (such as low college graduation rates) to reinsert themselves into the labor market and increase their assets. Many of them have relocated within the United States in search of new job opportunities.

How has the socioeconomic profile of Puerto Rican migrants changed over time?

The improved levels of schooling and occupational status of Puerto Rican migrants have attracted public attention over the past two decades. Journalists have sounded the alarm of a "brain drain," alleging that the loss of highly skilled human resources "bleeds" the Island's economy. Thousands of young university graduates have left their country because they cannot find employment commensurate with their academic qualifications, due to the Island's protracted recession. This export of talent has a high demographic and economic cost, by adding to an aging population and to the scarcity of personnel specializing in key areas of professional services such as health care and education. Between 2006 and 2016, the Medical Association of Puerto Rico reported a loss of 5,000 physicians, about 36 percent of its members, through migration.

Increasing numbers of middle-class Puerto Ricans have relocated abroad, seeking a better quality of life, including security, tranquility, health, housing, and education. The new migrants include a substantial proportion of teachers, nurses, engineers, and physicians, among other professionals. On average, the educational attainment of recent migrants surpasses that of those who migrated during the 1940s and 1950s, partly as a result of higher schooling levels in Puerto Rico. However, the contemporary exodus from the Island continues to draw primarily on people attracted by better employment, wages, and working conditions in the United States.

The latest census data confirm that recent Puerto Rican migrants have a relatively advantaged socioeconomic profile compared to earlier migrants. Nevertheless, contemporary migrants do not constitute a "brain drain" in the statistical sense of overrepresenting the better-educated sectors of the Island's population. According to census estimates, between the years 2010 and 2014, 9.8 percent of the migrants 25 years and over had completed a college education, compared to 17.4 percent on the Island. Only 3.8 percent had a graduate or professional degree, compared to 7.1 percent on the Island.

Census data also confirm that recent migrants underrepresent the higher occupational strata in Puerto Rico. Between 2010 and 2014, only 20.1 percent of employed migrants, compared to 31.3 percent of the Island's workers, were managers and professionals. The migrants had a slightly lower share (26 percent) of sales and office workers than Puerto Rico's labor force (28.8 percent). They also had a larger proportion (13.8 percent) of construction, maintenance, and repair workers than in Puerto Rico (10 percent). Overall, 53.9 percent of employed migrants were blue-collar and service workers, compared to 40 percent of the Island's labor force.

Such statistics suggest that the magnitude of the "brain drain" in Puerto Rico has been exaggerated. Therefore, the widespread notion that most people who have left the Island over the last decade are well-qualified professionals should be revised. Rather, the contemporary exodus comprises a cross section of Puerto Rican society, increasingly burdened by unemployment, poverty, and criminality. Today, most Puerto Rican migrants continue to be members of the working class, who are more likely to be unemployed and earn lower wages on the Island than abroad.

6

THE PUERTO RICAN DIASPORA TO THE UNITED STATES

CULTURE AND POLITICS

What is the Puerto Rican Day Parade?

The Puerto Rican Day Parade (*Desfile Puertorriqueño*) in New York City is the most visible display of Puerto Rican identity in the United States. The parade was first held in 1959 as an offshoot of the short-lived *Desfile Hispano*, organized in 1956 as an all-Hispanic festival. By the early 1960s, half a million Puerto Ricans watched their compatriots marching down Fifth Avenue in Manhattan.

Major community organizations and corporations now support the annual parade, many sponsoring *carrozas* (floats) with Puerto Rican motifs, such as the flag, folk music, and a beauty queen. Most Puerto Rican municipalities, as well as the Commonwealth government, participate in the event. Prominent Island figures have been appointed Grand Marshals, including former San Juan Mayor Felisa Rincón de Gautier (1897–1994), Independence Party President Rubén Berríos, New Progressive Party founder Luis A. Ferré, and Institute of Puerto Rican Culture founder Ricardo Alegría. In the year 2000, the parade was dedicated to the nationalist leader Pedro Albizu Campos, sparking protests from pro-statehood leaders in Puerto Rico. In 2016, the event organizers honored the political prisoner Oscar López Rivera and asked for his immediate release from prison. This year, the organizers estimated that 100,000 people marched and 1.5 million people attended the parade.

What is the role of religion within the Puerto Rican diaspora?

The mass migration of Puerto Ricans to the United States after World War II posed a challenge to the Catholic Church, particularly the Archdiocese of New York. Puerto Rican immigrants were impregnated with Catholic values and practices— but they were different from the prevailing ethos of the US Church, dominated by Irish Americans. Unlike Irish Catholics, Puerto Ricans brought with them few priests, nuns, and other religious personnel. In 1951, New York City did not have a single priest of Puerto Rican origin. Moreover, the Catholic Church no longer encouraged the establishment of "national parishes," as it previously had for Italian, German, and Polish immigrants. Instead, Catholic authorities preferred language-based integrated parishes, which added Spanish-language masses to regular services, usually in church basements. This policy required training non–Puerto Rican priests and nuns in the Spanish language and immersing them into Hispanic culture, sometimes in Puerto Rico itself. By 1961, New York City boasted forty-two Catholic parishes with Spanish-speaking priests (although only one was Puerto Rican).

Among the earliest organizations serving New York Puerto Ricans was the Catholic parish, *La Medalla Milagrosa* (Our Lady of the Miraculous Medal), founded in East Harlem in 1926 and closed down in the 1980s. The church continued to play a key role in welcoming Puerto Rican Catholics throughout the 1940s and 1950s. Other parishes that assisted the immigrants' spiritual needs included Our Lady of Providence in the Lower East Side of Manhattan and St. Luke's in the South Bronx.

Since 1953, New York Puerto Ricans commemorated the Feast of St. John the Baptist, the patron saint of the city of San Juan. The feast was first celebrated at La Milagrosa and sponsored by the Archdiocese of New York. By 1964, about sixty thousand Puerto Ricans attended an outdoor celebration in Randall's Island. Typically, the feast began with a procession and mass on June 24, the day of St. John the Baptist, followed by performances by choirs, bands, dance groups, and orchestras. Today, the Feast of St. John attracts fewer participants than the Puerto Rican Day Parade in New York.

Puerto Ricans in the United States have a relatively high share of Protestant followers. In 2015, the Pew Research Center found that 29 percent of US Puerto Ricans described themselves as Protestant, compared to 22 percent of all Hispanics. In a 2013 Pew poll, Puerto Ricans were more likely to identify as evangelical or Pentecostal (22 percent) than all Latinos (16 percent). Pentecostalism has spread rapidly among Puerto Rican immigrants and their descendants since the 1940s. By the early 1960s, New York City had at least 284 Protestant churches predominantly attended by Puerto Ricans. In 1968, Pentecostals had established as many as thirty storefront churches in Spanish Harlem. Today, most Pentecostal ministers and preachers within the Puerto Rican diaspora are of Puerto Rican origin.

Other religious practices include *espiritismo* (Spiritism) and *santería* (an Afro-Cuban religion). Puerto Ricans often consult a spiritual medium in times of distress. Many believe that spiritual disturbances can cause disease; that the spirits of the dead may manifest themselves directly in the daily lives of their close relatives; and that the two can communicate with each other. Spiritist practices, combined with folk remedies, are commonly used to heal both medical and psychological ailments. In an eclectic fashion, Puerto Rican Spiritism often incorporates the cult of the Catholic saints and the *orishas* (Yoruba deities) worshipped in *santería*. For many believers, Spiritism reduces the feelings of anxiety and depression, and strengthens their cultural identity and community belonging.

What is the role of the Spanish and English languages among Puerto Ricans in the United States?

Although many Puerto Rican immigrants still speak Spanish, an increasing number of their descendants have adopted English as their first language. Between 1980 and 2010, according to census data, English-speaking Puerto Rican households in the United States increased from 14.2 to 36.2 percent of all households, while Spanish-speaking households decreased from 85.2 to 63.4 percent. These figures corroborate that, over time, English inexorably replaces other languages spoken by immigrants and their descendants in the United States, usually within three generations. Puerto Ricans tend to follow the general pattern of the gradual loss of the immigrants' native language, although Spanish may survive longer than other languages in the United States. In 2010, two-thirds of the population of Puerto Rican origin in the United States still spoke Spanish. This linguistic persistence was more pronounced among first-generation immigrants than among their descendants.

The combination of Spanish and English, known pejoratively as "Spanglish," is increasingly common among Puerto Ricans and other Latinos in the United States. Many scholars initially thought that this practice impoverished and contaminated both languages. However, an increasing number of studies has reassessed how Puerto Ricans and other Hispanics switch between Spanish and English. Nowadays, many experts agree that so-called *code switching* (the alternation between linguistic codes) actually shows competence in more than one language and not a lack of ability in either of them. Rather than reflecting an intellectual or linguistic deficit, Spanglish may be considered a cultural asset, especially among second-generation immigrants, who usually have to communicate in both English and Spanish.

How did Puerto Rican literature develop in the United States?

The literature of the Puerto Rican diaspora has evolved in five main stages. The first phase, beginning in the last third of the nineteenth century, involved a cadre of political exiles in New York City, such as Eugenio María de Hostos, Ramón Emeterio Betances, Lola Rodríguez de Tió, Sotero Figueroa, and Arturo Alfonso Schomburg. During this stage, many Puerto Rican émigrés were committed to the Island's independence from Spain. Much of their writing was patriotic and propagandistic, and was transmitted primarily through letters, diaries, and newspaper articles, usually in the Spanish language.

A second moment in the literary history of New York Puerto Ricans was the arrival of thousands of skilled workers, especially cigar makers (*tabaqueros*), during the first two decades of the twentieth century. Bernardo Vega and Jesús Colón authored two of the most important memoirs of that period. Luisa Capetillo also wrote about her life in New York during the 1910s. Puerto Rican literature was then primarily journalistic and autobiographical, documenting the migrants' challenges and aspirations, such as learning English, organizing the community, and combating racial discrimination.

The third stage took place during the so-called Great Migration (1945–64). Island-born authors began to reflect upon the exodus to New York, including René Marqués, José Luis González, Emilio Díaz Valcárcel, Enrique Laguerre (1906–2005), and Julia de Burgos. Some of them personally experienced the migration process, but most remained close to the Island's literary canon. Many considered emigration as a serious threat to Puerto Rican identity, mainly through the loss of the Spanish vernacular. Most did not write from the migrants' standpoint and failed to capture the texture of their bilingual and bicultural communities. An exception to this trend is Pedro Juan Soto, a New York–born novelist who returned to Puerto Rico in the 1950s.

The fourth stage began in the mid-1960s and is associated with Miguel Algarín (b. 1941) and Miguel Piñero (1946–88), who cofounded the Nuyorican Poets Café in 1973 in the Lower East Side of Manhattan. Other authors identified with the Nuyorican movement include its literary precursor Piri

Thomas (1930–2011), Pedro Pietri (1944–2004), Tato Laviera (1950–2013), and Sandra María Esteves. Their writing featured autobiographical references, the predominance of the English language, street slang, realism, subversive politics, and a rupture with the Island's literary models. Nuyorican writers often articulated a mythical image of Puerto Rico and its African and indigenous roots. They shared much with other minority writers, especially African Americans and Chicanos, in their protest against racial and class oppression, ethnic affirmation, nonstandard language, and search for new forms of expression. The Nuyorican movement defied the Island-centered canon in literature, especially through its preference for English and its creative mixture with Spanish.

Beginning in the 1980s, the fifth stage of Puerto Rican literature in the United States has been dubbed "post-Nuyorican" or "diasporican" (following the sobriquet coined by the Bronx-born poet María Teresa "Mariposa" Fernández, b. 1974). Some authors, such as Edward Rivera (1944–2001), Esmeralda Santiago (b. 1948), and Judith Ortiz Coffer (b. 1952), continue to rely on autobiographical narratives. Others, such as Ed Vega (1936–2008), Nicholasa Mohr (b. 1938), and Abraham Rodríguez (b. 1961), write short stories and novels about growing up Puerto Rican in the United States. Santiago, Ortiz Coffer, and Aurora Levins Morales (b. 1954) have moved away from the Nuyorican movement's emphasis on urban blight, violence, colloquialism, and radicalism. Some of the recent changes in Puerto Rican writing in the United States are part of the "mainstreaming" of ethnic literature, as well as a small boom in Latino literature since the 1990s.

What is the Nuyorican Poets Café?

For more than four decades, the Nuyorican Poets Café has provided a key venue for public performances of poetry, music, theater, and the visual arts. It began as an informal gathering for Puerto Rican writers and artists in the living room of Miguel Algarín's East Village apartment. After renting an old Irish pub between 1975 and 1980, the organizers moved the café to its present location in a small renovated warehouse in the Lower East Side of Manhattan. Its founders appropriated the term "Nuyorican," which had previously been used as a derogatory reference to the Puerto Rican diaspora.

Many of the café's original members—such as Piñero, Bimbo Rivas (1939–92), Esteves, and Laviera—made the Lower East Side neighborhood (now known as *Loisaida*) the subject of their literature. Much of their poetry chronicled and denounced the social problems of New York's inner-city *barrios*, such as poverty, crime, and drug addiction. At the same time, Nuyorican poetry was also a sign of collective affirmation amid adverse circumstances. Since the mid-1970s, the café has promoted several generations of Nuyorican poets, from the pioneering Pietri and Víctor Hernández Cruz (b. 1949), to the more recent work of Caridad de la Luz ("La Bruja," b. 1977) and "Mariposa" Fernández.

Today, the Nuyorican Poets Café is a well-established nonprofit organization that attracts an ethnically and racially diverse audience. Since the mid-1990s, the institution has distanced itself from its nationalist beginnings and adopted a more transnational approach, appealing to a multicultural set of performers and spectators. In addition to poetry slams, the café regularly features open-mic competitions, hip hop, Latin jazz, and film screenings. Many of the café's current artists, staff members, board of directors, and audience members are not Puerto Rican, such as African Americans and Asian Americans. Cofounder Algarín still belongs to the board of directors of the institution, which remains anchored in New York's Puerto Rican and Latino community. A Nuyorican Café opened in Old San Juan in 1973, as a night club combining art, music, theater, and food, but focusing on salsa dancing rather than poetry recitals.

What is the "flying bus"?

"The Flying Bus" (*la guagua aérea*) is the title of a 1983 short story by the Puerto Rican writer Luis Rafael Sánchez, as well as its 1993 film adaptation directed by Luis Molina Casanova (b. 1951). It has become the best-known literary image for circular migration between the Island and the US mainland. Sánchez's narrative takes place aboard the cheap late-night flight between the San Juan and New York airports. The text suggests that Puerto Ricans shuttle between the two places as if they were just taking a brief bus ride. For the Puerto Rican passengers of the flying bus, traveling to or from New York is like jumping across a pond (*brincar el charco*). As one character quips, "*I live with one leg in New York and the other in Puerto Rico.*"

Sánchez's powerful allegory of a flying bus helps to revise the standard notion of migration as a permanent change of residence with an irrevocable shift in identity. As the literary critic Hugo Rodríguez Vecchini has pointed out, contemporary Puerto Rican migration exceeds the conventional connotations of the term "migration," including moving, visiting, traveling, commuting, and going back and forth. Thus, Sánchez's text proposes that being Puerto Rican is no longer a matter of living here or there, in Puerto Rico or in the United States. It is rather a question of how a person defines herself subjectively, like the passenger in the flying bus who claims she comes from the town of "New York, Puerto Rico."

How did Puerto Rican music emerge in the United States?

During the first half of the twentieth century, many Puerto Rican musicians moved to New York City, including the famous composer Rafael Hernández (1892–1965), bandleader Pedro Flores (1894–1979), and singer Manuel "Canario" Jiménez (1895–1975). These musicians helped articulate the cultural identity of their diasporic communities as well as their homeland. It was in Spanish Harlem that Hernández wrote

Puerto Rico's unofficial anthem, *Lamento borincano* (Puerto Rican Lament), in 1929. It was also in New York that "Canario" recorded the first *plenas* for RCA Victor in the 1920s. Between 1925 and 1945, most of the major Puerto Rican composers (including Noro Morales [1912–63] and Bobby Capó [1922–89], as well as Hernández and Flores) were living in New York City. Noel Estrada (1918–79) also wrote his nostalgic ode to Puerto Rican migration, *En mi Viejo San Juan* (In My Old San Juan), in the 1940s.

New York Puerto Ricans preserved much of their country music (*música jíbara*), especially as played by guitar-and-voice trios. Although Afro-Cuban genres—from *rumba* to *mambo* to *cha-cha-chá*—gradually became synonymous with Latin music, Puerto Ricans often performed in Latin orchestras and bands. Along with African Americans and Cubans, they also contributed to the development of Latin jazz during the 1930s and 1940s. By the 1950s and 1960s, New York Puerto Ricans were involved in a series of short-lived musical fads, such as *pachanga* and *bugalú*.

In the 1970s, Puerto Ricans participated actively in the emerging salsa music scene in New York City. According to some experts, salsa originated in the musical circuit linking Puerto Ricans between New York and San Juan since the beginning of the twentieth century. According to others, salsa was merely a convenient way to market old-style Cuban music in the United States. In any case, when the Fania record company began to market salsa in the late 1960s, it was geared primarily toward the so-called Nuyoricans. Although Puerto Ricans in the US mainland and the Island remain among salsa's most faithful followers, the music has become widely heard among other US Latinos, such as Cubans in Miami and Dominicans in New York. Salsa's leading performers have included Puerto Ricans Willie Colón (b. 1950) and Héctor Lavoe (1946–93), Dominican Johnny Pacheco (b. 1935), and Cuban Celia Cruz (1925–2003), as well as Panamanian Rubén Blades (b. 1948), Venezuelan Oscar D'León (b. 1943), and Colombian Julio

Ernesto Estrada ("Fruko," b. 1951). Today, salsa is an emblem of a broad Latino identity throughout the Americas, Europe, and elsewhere; it has become part of "world music."

During the early 1970s, young Puerto Ricans contributed to the rise of a hip hop subculture in the South Bronx. Although rap music was later labeled as "black," Puerto Ricans retain a strong presence in the "hip hop zone." Hip hop has remained a critical site of cultural production for second- and third-generation Puerto Ricans as well as African Americans. New York Puerto Rican hip hoppers negotiate the boundaries of Puerto Ricanness, Latinoness, and blackness through rhymes that privilege the English language and particularly African American linguistic practices. Since the late 1990s, code switching between English and Spanish has been increasingly common among Puerto Rican rappers.

Today, the most popular musical expression among Puerto Rican youth, both in the United States and in Puerto Rico, is *reggaetón*, which combines reggae, rap, and other African American and Caribbean genres. Most of the artists who participate in the *reggaetón* scene were born and raised on the Island and are Spanish dominant. Some of the genre's performers have successfully crossed over into the English-speaking market, such as Daddy Yankee and Wisin & Yandel.

To what extent do US Puerto Ricans identify as Hispanic or Latino?

At first sight, Puerto Ricans are Hispanic or Latino almost by default, because they can trace their origin to a Spanish-speaking country. Furthermore, Puerto Ricans are the second largest group of US Latinos after Mexicans, which together constitute the prototypes of the Hispanic category popularized since the 1970s. According to the US Census, the terms "Hispanic" or "Latino" refer to persons of Cuban, Mexican, Puerto Rican, South or Central American, or other Spanish culture or origin, regardless of race. More broadly, *Latinidad* (Latinoness) or *Hispanidad* (Hispanicity) suggests that, despite their differences, the peoples originating in Latin America share a similar geographic, historical, cultural, and linguistic background. However, the Hispanic/Latino classification lumps together a wide variety of immigrant histories, colonial legacies, racial and ethnic groups, social classes, cultural practices, languages, and dialects. Thus, Puerto Ricans should not be subsumed under a label that silences such fundamental differences with other populations.

A 2013 survey conducted by the Pew Research Center asked US Latinos how they preferred to describe their identities. About 54 percent identified themselves most often by their place of origin, using such terms as Mexican, Puerto Rican, or Cuban; only 20 percent chose Hispanic or Latino. Another 23 percent of the interviewees said they used the term "American" most often to describe themselves. Among Puerto Rican respondents, 55 percent preferred to identify themselves by national origin, while only 14 percent favored the pan-ethnic terms "Hispanic" or "Latino," and 28 percent used "American" most often, a higher share than among any other Latino group. The hyphenated term "Puerto Rican-American" may be considered redundant, since all Puerto Ricans are US citizens by birth.

How have the US media traditionally represented Puerto Ricans?

Since the mid-1940s, Puerto Ricans in the United States—especially in New York City—have been publicly depicted as a "social problem"—from creating housing shortages and overcrowded schools to increasing unemployment, crime, and welfare dependence. They have also been stereotyped because of their dark skin color, foreign language and culture, rural background, low educational status, and lack of occupational skills. Consequently, Puerto Ricans have often been stigmatized as lazy, ignorant, violent, sexually obsessed, physically unfit, culturally deficient, and dark-skinned aliens (despite their US citizenship).

Broadway musicals and Hollywood movies, from *West Side Story* (1957/1961) to *The Capeman* (1998), particularly gang films such as *Fort Apache, the Bronx* (1981), *Q and A* (1990), and *Carlito's Way* (1993), have disseminated disparaging views of Puerto Ricans. Some episodes of prime-time television programs such as *Seinfeld* (1998) and *Law and Order* (2001) have also featured defamatory references to New York Puerto Ricans. This negative media portrayal is common among working-class immigrants and racial minorities in the United States and elsewhere.

The best-known representation of stateside Puerto Ricans remains *West Side Story*. Both the stage and film versions portray Puerto Ricans as inherently musical, sexualized, racialized, and criminal subjects. The plot line pits the dark-skinned Sharks, a Puerto Rican teenage gang from the Upper West Side of Manhattan, against the light-skinned Jets, composed of the children of European immigrants, perhaps Italians. The impossible romance between the Puerto Rican Maria and the unspecified white ethnic, Tony, unleashes a violent confrontation between the two rival gangs for control of the territory. This modern version of the Romeo and Juliet narrative envisions Puerto Ricans as racial and ethnic outsiders to the Anglo-American mainstream. Like previous waves of immigrants, Puerto Ricans are expected to assimilate into the "American way of life" or remain marginalized. After *West Side Story*, many other US motion pictures have depicted Puerto Ricans through enduring ethnic and racial clichés.

Until recently, Puerto Rican (and more generally Hispanic) roles in commercial films were limited to a few standard characters, such as the hot-blooded vamp or spitfire, the exotic dark lady, the male or female clown, the stupid greaser, the treacherous bandit, the swarthy Latin lover, and the smooth gentleman. Even today, Hollywood typecasts most Hispanic actors and actresses in one of these roles, often in stereotyped depictions of urban violence and loose morals, focusing on juvenile gangs, drug trafficking, and sexual promiscuity. Despite

the emergence of a small independent Hispanic film industry, Latinos are still largely invisible in the English-language
media. Latinos, and particularly Puerto Ricans, have fared
worse in network television than other racial and ethnic minorities such as African Americans and Asian Americans, who
have recently improved their coverage.

How did the Puerto Rican diaspora become incorporated into US politics?

Puerto Ricans have established numerous voluntary associations in the United States since the late nineteenth century.
Between 1920 and 1945, they founded at least three dozen
organizations in New York City alone. Immigrants often
adapted Island-based institutions such as labor unions, hometown clubs, Masonic lodges, and political parties. By 1960,
around three hundred community organizations were active
in New York City. By far the most common form of association
was the hometown club, grouping a small clique of relatives
and friends from the same locality on the Island. Most of these
groups called themselves *ausentes* (the absent ones) or *hijos*
(sons and daughters) of a town back home. By 1961, all of the
Island's seventy-eight municipalities were represented among
the city's clubs.

Some of the earliest community organizations founded by
Puerto Ricans in New York and New Jersey were oriented
toward US politics. A Porto Rican Democratic Club was estab-
lished in Brooklyn in 1922. Two other Democratic clubs, the
Guaybana and Betances, were organized in the late 1920s. In
1937, Oscar García Rivera (1900–69) became the first Puerto
Rican elected official in the United States, as a Republican rep-
resenting East Harlem to the New York State Assembly. After
World War II, many Puerto Ricans joined the Democratic Party.
They also created their own nonprofit institutions, such as the
Puerto Rican Day Parade organization, established in 1958;
ASPIRA, a high-school advocacy program founded by social

worker Antonia Pantoja (1922–2002), sociologist Frank Bonilla (1925–2010), and others in 1961; and the National Association for Puerto Rican Civil Rights (NAPRCR, 1964), led by Gilberto Gerena Valentín (1918–2016).

Since the 1950s, second-generation immigrants began to claim a separate ethnic identity, combining cultural nationalism with the rhetoric of the civil rights movement. This distinctive sense of identity emerged largely in response to a new ideology of cultural pluralism and later antipoverty programs in the United States. Many New York Puerto Rican activists were radicalized during the 1960s, especially as a result of the Vietnam War and the Black Power movement. Several left-wing groups were active in the US mainland, including the Young Lords and the Puerto Rican Socialist Party.

The number of Puerto Rican community organizations grew since the mid-1960s as a result of new funding opportunities available through War on Poverty programs and the rise of a generation of college-educated professionals who advocated politically for the community's needs. Grassroots movements of various ideological persuasions mobilized Puerto Ricans to demand public recognition in cities such as New York City, Chicago, Philadelphia, and Hartford. Today, dozens of voluntary associations represent different sectors of the diaspora—from professionals and scholars to merchants and civil servants. More than one hundred organizations are currently affiliated with the National Puerto Rican Coalition, a policy-oriented lobbying group based in Washington, DC, and founded in 1977.

Puerto Ricans have become increasingly involved in US electoral politics, especially as part of the Democratic Party. In 1970, Herman Badillo (1929–2014) was the first Puerto Rican elected to the US House of Representatives, where he served for three consecutive terms. During the 1990s, three Puerto Rican Democrats joined the US House of Representatives—José E. Serrano (b. 1943), Nydia Velázquez (b. 1953), and Luis Gutiérrez (b. 1953)—and are still serving in Congress, together with Puerto Rico's resident commissioner (currently Jenniffer González, b. 1976). Raúl Labrador (b. 1967), a Republican, was elected as a US representative in 2011. In 1999, there were ninety-five elected officials of Puerto Rican ancestry in the municipal, state, and federal spheres of the US government. By 2004, the figure had increased to 150. Puerto Ricans are well represented in the legislatures of states such as New York, New Jersey, and Connecticut. In 2012, the New York City Council had eight officials of Puerto Rican origin, including Melissa Mark-Viverito (b. 1969), who was elected speaker in 2014. Overall, Puerto Ricans in the United States have attained a relatively high level of political representation, although they remain underrepresented in proportion to their numbers.

Who is Sonia Sotomayor?

Sonia Sotomayor (b. 1954) is the first person of Puerto Rican and Latin American ancestry to serve as Associate Justice of the US Supreme Court. Born in New York City of Puerto Rican parents who migrated during World War II, she grew up within a working-class family in a public housing project in the South Bronx. Sotomayor earned a bachelor's degree in history (*summa cum laude*) from Princeton University in 1976 and a law degree from Yale University in 1979.

Upon graduating from law school, Sotomayor was appointed assistant district attorney in Manhattan between 1979 and 1984. She then joined a private law firm in New York, where she became a partner in 1988. She was named judge on the US District Court for the Southern District of Manhattan in 1992 and became well-known for her judicial decision to "save baseball" in a 1995 dispute between Major League team owners and players. In 1998 she was confirmed as a judge on the US Court of Appeals for the Second Circuit and, in 2009, she became the first Hispanic and the third woman on the US Supreme Court. As a Supreme Court Justice, she has been closely identified with legal debates related to race, ethnicity, and gender. On most social, economic, and political matters—ranging from abortion and gay marriage to affirmative action and gun control—she has accumulated a moderately liberal record.

Who is Oscar López Rivera?

Born in 1943 in San Sebastián, Puerto Rico, Oscar López Rivera is one of the political prisoners who has served the longest sentences—more than thirty-five years now—in the United States and the world. He moved with his family to Chicago in 1957 and finished high school there. During the 1960s, he developed a radical political position regarding Puerto Rico, embracing nationalism and socialism. At least since 1976, he became associated with the Armed Forces of National Liberation (*Fuerzas Armadas de Liberación Nacional*, or FALN), a clandestine paramilitary organization that claimed the bombing of military, government, and banking institutions in the United States. In 1981, López Rivera was charged with seditious conspiracy against the US government, armed robbery, and other charges. He was sentenced to fifty-five years of imprisonment and received an additional fifteen years for conspiracy to escape from prison in 1988.

Considered a "terrorist" by some and a "freedom fighter" by others, López Rivera has received broad support for clemency from leaders of various political affiliations in the United States and Puerto Rico. They include former President Jimmy Carter, Senator Bernie Sanders, the three Puerto Rican members of Congress (Luis Gutiérrez, José Serrano, and Nydia Velásquez), former Resident Commissioner Pedro Pierluisi, former Governor Alejandro García Padilla, San Juan Mayor Carmen Yulín Cruz, and former Governor Aníbal Acevedo Vilá. In addition, the campaign has drawn a large following within Puerto Rico's civil society and human rights organizations. López Rivera's portrait can now be seen in many public places throughout the Island, especially in the streets of Old San Juan. As of December 2016, President Barack Obama has not responded to the plea to "bring Oscar back home."

How do most stateside Puerto Ricans vote in US elections?

Most Puerto Ricans in the United States are affiliated with the Democratic Party, and most Puerto Rican elected officials are Democrats. Puerto Ricans now constitute one of the most solid blocs of Democratic voters, along with African Americans and Mexican Americans. A 2012 nationwide poll led by Professor Eduardo Gamarra found that 71.3 percent of stateside Puerto Ricans identified as Democrats, while only 22.8 percent said they were Republican. In recent presidential elections, Puerto Ricans have overwhelmingly favored Democratic candidates, from Bill Clinton to Barack Obama. The vast majority of Puerto Ricans (as well as most Latinos) voted for Hillary Clinton in November 2016.

The Democratic Party, however, did not initially welcome Puerto Ricans in New York City as well as other ethnic groups, such as the Irish, Italians, and Jews. Nor did the Republican Party pay much attention to the Puerto Rican electorate until the mid-twentieth century. Over time, Puerto Ricans became a major force in Democratic political machines in cities such as New York, Chicago, Philadelphia, Boston, and Hartford. In 1978, approximately 82 percent of Puerto Ricans in New York City voted for the Democratic Party and only 11 percent for the Republican Party. Historically, Puerto Ricans have shown a stronger ideological affinity with the Democratic Party because of its support for the expansion of government programs for the poor, especially in education and health care. To this day, Puerto Ricans in the United States tend to back Democratic candidates who espouse liberal public policies.

What is the role of the Puerto Rican diaspora in solving the Island's status issue?

The contribution of stateside Puerto Ricans to determining the Island's political future is still under dispute. Until now, all local elections, referenda, and plebiscites have been restricted to Island residents. Nonetheless, Puerto Ricans in the United States have reiterated their desire to participate in the definition of the political future of their country of origin. More recently, they have expressed strong concerns about the Island's economic downturn. In July 2016, a group of stateside elected officials and community leaders established the National Puerto Rican Agenda (NPRA), a nonpartisan coalition focusing on the Island's current fiscal crisis.

It is difficult to assess the ideological preferences of stateside Puerto Ricans, compared to those of Island residents. Although outdated, a 2004 public poll sponsored by the newspaper *El Nuevo Día* found that 48 percent of Puerto Ricans in Central Florida favored Commonwealth status, while 42 percent preferred the Island's annexation as a state of the union, and 5 percent supported independence. A more recent poll, conducted by the Center for American Progress Action Fund and Latino Decisions in September 2016, found that 56 percent of Puerto Ricans in Florida favored statehood. Meanwhile, only 25 percent favored Commonwealth status and 8 percent supported independence (the remaining 12 percent did not have a strong opinion on the issue). In any case, Puerto Ricans living in the United States have never participated in a plebiscite on the status of Puerto Rico. The ill-fated Puerto Rico Democracy Act of 2010 (H.R. 2499), a bill sponsored by former Resident Commissioner Pierluisi, would have extended the right to vote to US residents born on the Island. But the bill was never approved by the Senate. It is unlikely that the diaspora's participation would radically alter a plebiscite's results in Puerto Rico.

EPILOGUE

The cover image for this book—a colorful photograph of Old San Juan by Joe Raedle—features a balcony with a Puerto Rican flag hanging next to a "For Sale" (*Se Vende*) sign. Is it just the colonial-style apartment that is for sale or is it the entire Island metaphorically as well? Consider that property values in Puerto Rico have plunged 28 percent since the real estate bubble in 2008. Total housing sales have since continued to drop, and the Island's housing stock has become a buyer's market. The average price of a new home in Puerto Rico ($153,442) in February 2016 was 10.3 percent less than a year before. In 2015, the Island recorded the second highest number of foreclosures (4,459) of any state or US jurisdiction, after New Jersey. Largely due to massive outmigration to the US mainland, 22.3 percent of all housing units on the Island were vacant in 2015, up from 13.7 percent in 2006. Much of Puerto Rico is literally for sale.

Puerto Rico's Planning Board currently projects that positive rates of economic growth on the Island will not resume until after 2017. Full economic recovery could take a decade longer, given the Island's gigantic public debt and other structural problems of the economy, especially after the demise of federal tax incentives under Section 936. Even under the most optimistic scenario, Puerto Rico's Gross Domestic Product (GDP) is likely to stagnate in the near future.

Similarly, the US Census Bureau forecasts that Puerto Rico's population will decline steadily at least until 2050. The combination of low birth and death rates will expand an already aging population. Correspondingly, large-scale migration to the United States, particularly among the younger sectors of the population, will probably persist in the short- to medium-term. It is more difficult to predict what changes, if any, will occur in the Island's political status. Much depends on how PROMESA—the Puerto Rico Oversight, Management, and Economic Stability Act of 2016—affects the political party system and prevailing ideological currents on the Island. In the end, it is up to Congress to initiate a binding process of consultation with the Puerto Rican people about their political future.

As if the Island's economic and political prospects were not bleak enough, on September 21, 2016, a massive power outage left 1.5 million households and businesses without electricity. The government-run electrical company could not immediately determine the cause of a fire at the Aguirre power station in southern Puerto Rico, which led to the collapse of the entire electrical system. Governor García Padilla declared a state of emergency on the Island, but denied that poor maintenance and outdated equipment had triggered the blackout. Restoring power throughout the Island took several days.

Amid the distressing media coverage of Puerto Rico, a ray of light shone when Mónica Puig won the gold medal in women's tennis singles at the summer 2016 Olympic Games in Rio de Janeiro, Brazil. This unexpected athletic victory helped instill an optimistic mood on the Island and wherever Puerto Ricans live across the United States. Multitudinous celebrations, both spontaneous and official, took place in San Juan and throughout the Island. Puerto Rico's national anthem, *La Borinqueña*, was played and the single-starred flag was hoisted for the first time in Olympic history. For many Puerto Ricans on and off the Island, Puig's personal accomplishment had a broader meaning of collective hope and resiliency against all odds. As Puig declared after winning the Olympic championship, "I think I united a nation, and I just love where I come from."

SUGGESTIONS FOR FURTHER READING

Acosta-Belén, Edna, and Carlos E. Santiago. *Puerto Ricans in the United States: A Contemporary Portrait*. Boulder, CO: Lynne Rienner, 2006.

Acosta Cruz, María. *Dream Nation: Puerto Rican Culture and the Fictions of Independence*. New Brunswick, NJ: Rutgers University Press, 2014.

Aranda, Elizabeth M. *Emotional Bridges to Puerto Rico: Migration, Return Migration, and the Struggles of Incorporation*. Lanham, MD: Rowman & Littlefield, 2007.

Ayala, César A., and Rafael Bernabe. *Puerto Rico in the American Century: A History since 1898*. Chapel Hill: University of North Carolina Press, 2009.

Bosque-Pérez, Ramón, and José Javier Colón, eds. *Puerto Rico under Colonial Rule: Political Persecution and the Quest for Human Rights*. Albany: State University of New York Press, 2006.

Briggs, Laura. *Reproducing Empire: Race, Sex, Science, and U.S. Imperialism in Puerto Rico*. Berkeley: University of California Press, 2002.

Burnett, Christina Duffy, and Burke Marshall, eds. *Foreign in a Domestic Sense: Puerto Rico, American Expansion, and the Constitution*. Durham, NC: Duke University Press, 2001.

Cabán, Pedro. *Constructing a Colonial People: Puerto Rico and the United States, 1898–1932*. Boulder, CO: Westview, 1999.

Chinea, Jorge Luis. *Race and Labor in the Hispanic Caribbean: The West Indian Immigrant Experience in Puerto Rico, 1800–1850*. Gainesville: University Press of Florida, 2005.

Dávila, Arlene M. *Sponsored Identities: Cultural Politics in Puerto Rico*. Philadelphia: Temple University Press, 1997.

Del Moral, Solsiree. *Negotiating Empire: The Cultural Politics of Schools in Puerto Rico, 1898–1952*. Madison: University of Wisconsin Press, 2013.

Dietz, James L. *Puerto Rico: Negotiating Development and Change*. Boulder, CO: Lynne Rienner, 2003.

Duany, Jorge. *The Puerto Rican Nation on the Move: Identities on the Island and in the United States*. Chapel Hill: University of North Carolina Press, 2002.

Duany, Jorge, and Félix V. Matos-Rodríguez. *Puerto Ricans in Orlando and Central Florida*. New York: Centro de Estudios Puertorriqueños, Hunter College, City University of New York, 2006.

Figueroa, Luis A. *Sugar, Slavery, and Freedom in Nineteenth-Century Puerto Rico*. Chapel Hill: University of North Carolina Press, 2005.

Findlay, Eileen Suárez. *Imposing Decency: The Politics of Sexuality and Race in Puerto Rico, 1870–1920*. Durham, NC: Duke University Press, 2001.

Flores, Juan. *The Diaspora Strikes Back: Caribeño Tales of Learning and Turning*. New York: Routledge, 2009.

Font-Guzmán, Jacqueline N. *Experiencing Puerto Rican Citizenship and Cultural Nationalism*. New York: Palgrave Macmillan, 2015.

Godreau, Isar P. *Scripts of Blackness: Race, Cultural Nationalism, and U.S. Colonialism in Puerto Rico*. Urbana: University of Illinois Press, 2015.

Grosfoguel, Ramón. *Colonial Subjects: Puerto Ricans in a Global Perspective*. Berkeley: University of California Press, 2003.

Guerra, Lillian. *Popular Expression and National Identity in Puerto Rico: The Struggle for Self, Community, and Nation*. Gainesville: University Press of Florida, 1998.

Haslip-Viera, Gabriel, ed. *Taíno Revival: Critical Perspectives on Puerto Rican Identity and Cultural Politics*. Princeton, NJ: Markus Wiener, 2001.

La Fountain-Stokes, Lawrence. *Queer Ricans: Culture and Sexualities in the Diaspora*. Minneapolis: University of Minnesota Press, 2009.

Levy, Teresita A. *Puerto Ricans in the Empire: Tobacco Growers and U.S. Colonialism*. New Brunswick, NJ: Rutgers University Press, 2015.

Lloréns, Hilda. *Imaging the Great Puerto Rican Family: Framing Nation, Race, and Gender during the American Century*. Lanham, MD: Lexington, 2014.

López, Iris. *Matters of Choice: Puerto Rican Women's Struggle for Reproductive Freedom*. New Brunswick, NJ: Rutgers University Press, 2008.

Meléndez, Edwin, and Carlos Ramos-Vargas, ed. *Puerto Ricans at the Dawn of the New Millennium*. New York: Center for Puerto Rican Studies, 2014.

Moreno, Marisel C. *Family Matters: Puerto Rican Women Authors on the Island and the Mainland*. Charlottesville: University of Virginia Press, 2012.

Morris, Nancy. *Puerto Rico: Culture, Politics, and Identity*. Westport, CT: Praeger, 1995.

Negrón-Muntaner, Frances. *Boricua Pop: Puerto Ricans and the Latinization of American Culture*. New York: New York University Press, 2004.

Negrón-Muntaner, Frances, ed. *None of the Above: Puerto Ricans in the Global Era*. New York: Palgrave Macmillan, 2007.

Ortiz Cuadra, Cruz Miguel. *Eating Puerto Rico: A History of Food, Culture, and Identity*. Chapel Hill: University of North Carolina Press, 2013.

Pérez, Gina M. *The Near Northwest Side Story: Migration, Displacement, and Puerto Rican Families*. Berkeley: University of California Press, 2004.

Picó, Fernando. *History of Puerto Rico: A Panorama of Its People*. Princeton, NJ: Markus Wiener, 2006.

Ramos-Zayas, Ana Y. *National Performances: The Politics of Class, Race, and Space in Puerto Rican Chicago*. Chicago: University of Chicago Press, 2003.

Rivera, Raquel Z. *Nuyoricans from the Hip Hop Zone*. New York: Palgrave Macmillan, 2003.

Rivera, Raquel Z., Wayne Marshall, and Deborah Pacini Hernández, eds. *Reggaeton*. Durham, NC: Duke University Press, 2009.

Rivera Ramos, Efrén. *The Legal Construction of Identity: The Judicial and Social Legacy of American Colonialism in Puerto Rico*. Washington, DC: American Psychological Association, 2001.

Rivero, Yeidy M. *Tuning Out Blackness: Race and Nation in the History of Puerto Rican Television*. Durham, NC: Duke University Press, 2005.

Rodríguez Beruff, Jorge. *Strategy as Politics: Puerto Rico on the Eve of the Second World War*. Río Piedras, PR: La Editorial, Universidad de Puerto Rico, 2007.

Romberg, Raquel. *Witchcraft and Welfare: Spiritual Capital and the Business of Magic in Modern Puerto Rico*. Austin: University of Texas Press, 2003.

Rouse, Irving. *The Taínos: Rise and Decline of the People Who Greeted Columbus*. New Haven, CT: Yale University Press, 1992.

Roy-Féquière, Magali. *Women, Creole Identity, and Intellectual Life in Early Twentieth-Century Puerto Rico*. Philadelphia: Temple University Press, 2004.

Soto-Crespo, Ramón E. *Mainland Passage: The Cultural Anomaly of Puerto Rico*. Minneapolis: University of Minnesota Press, 2009.

Sotomayor, Antonio. *The Sovereign Colony: Olympic Sport, National Identity, and International Politics in Puerto Rico*. Lincoln: University of Nebraska Press, 2016.

Thomas, Lorrin. *Puerto Rican Citizen: History and Political Identity in Twentieth-Century New York City*. Chicago: University of Chicago Press, 2010.

Thompson, Lanny. *Imperial Archipelago: Representation and Rule in the Insular Territories under U.S. Dominion after 1898*. Honolulu: University of Hawai'i Press, 2010.

Torres-Padilla, José L., and Carmen Haydée Rivera, eds. *Writing Off the Hyphen: New Critical Perspectives on the Literature of the Puerto Rican Diaspora*. Seattle: University of Washington Press, 2008.

Whalen, Carmen Teresa, and Víctor Vázquez-Hernández, eds. *The Puerto Rican Diaspora: Historical Perspectives*. Philadelphia: Temple University Press, 2005.

INDEX